Golden Rule Civility

An Action Plan for Building a Global Culture of Honor

Dr. Lew Bayer and Dr. Clyde Rivers

CONTENTS

ABOUT THIS BOOK

Welcome to *Golden Rule Civility*. This book is intended as a "think" book. The content is based on aspects of <u>The Golden Rule Civility Global Initiative</u> which is a collaborative worldwide project co-created by iChange Nations Inc. and Civility Experts Inc. Recent strategic partners in the Initiative also include The National Civility Center and The International Civility Trainers' Consortium.

The initiative is focused on building a global culture of honor. Through its efforts, The Golden Rule Civility Global Initiative strives to convey the idea that each of us, each individual, is responsible for doing his/her part to make the world a better, kinder, more civil place. By acknowledging and utilizing the gifts that each of us has to offer, we can work together through our collaborations and contributions to create homes, communities, and workplaces where adherence to The Golden Rule Philosophy of treating other how you would like to be treated, drives our decision-making. In addition, a secondary focus of the Initiative is to provide tools and supports for building the skills that underpin the ability to exhibit civility and live by the Golden Rule. These skills are critical to building cultures of honor.

Throughout the book, key concepts related to Golden Rule Civility are introduced and discussed. The co-authors' hope is that you will not only take time to learn these concepts - some of which may be brand new to you – but that you will also take time to think about:

- How you can apply these concepts to your own way of thinking?
- How you can live The Golden Rule in your own day-to-day life?
- How you can build competency in civility-oriented skills?
- How you can interact with others in a more civil way?
- How you can move forward as an ambassador for change and lead others by example?
- How can you raise awareness about how each of us shares in the global responsibility to build cultures of honor?
- In what specific and intentional way will you use your personal gifts to make a difference?

As the first step to meeting our moral and ethical obligations to fulfill our individual responsibility to ourselves and to each other, **please be sure to complete your personal Golden Rule Civility Action Plan** (you'll find it at the end of the book.) Remember, just talking about change- and/or just thinking about kindness- this isn't enough. We each need to commit to taking even some small deliberate action toward changing behavior and people treatment. We need to adhere to personal codes of honor and to work together to build global cultures of honor.

If you are studying to be a Global Golden Rule Civility Statesman, or a Global Golden Rule Civility Master Statesman, this book offers a useful, practical tool where you can record your thoughts and insights.

OVERVIEW OF THE KEY CONCEPTS

"We will reframe the world with honor"- Dr. Clyde Rivers

The key concepts included in this book represent just a few of the core ideas and strategies that make up The Golden Rule Civility Global Initiative. For a comprehensive listing and/or to learn more, to attend a Golden Rule Civility presentation in a city near you, or to train to become a Golden Rule Civility Statesman, please visit the Resources section at the end of the book.

The key concepts are ordered in the way you would need to gain the knowledge, e.g., the concepts build on each other. It is recommended that you start with Key Concept 1 and work your way through to Key Concept 10.

Key Concept 1: The Golden Rule
Key Concept 2: Civility
Key Concept 3: Golden Rule Civility
Key Concept 4: Collaboration
Key Concept 5: End in Mind Thinking
Key Concept 6: Culture of Honor
Key Concept 7: Golden Rule Civility Statesmen
Key Concept 8: Interruption Strategies
Key Concept 9: The Golden Rule Question
Key Concept 10: Golden Rule Dialogue

INTRODUCTION

There are amazing contributions within everyone born on this earth. When those contributions are brought forth in individuals and these individuals are honored for their addition to humanity and our world, the world becomes a better place. For many years, the work that Dr. Clyde Rivers, and the team at iChange Nations Inc. (ICN), have engaged in is grounded in the belief that every life is valuable and created with a specific purpose and gift. It is not good to overlook greatness in others. If we do, we starve as humankind on the earth, we create a "gift famine". Gifts that would be solving our problems and enhancing our world are potentially lost when we diminish, dismiss, or destroy others- whether emotional, spiritually, or physically. The ICN team is committed to raising awareness about the consequences of dishonor and to changing the fundamental way people all around the world treat each other.

All we have to do is look around to see that we are experiencing a crisis of conscience and civility. Whether it's employees experiencing incivility in the workplace an average of 8.5

times   per week[1], 43% of our young people (Millennials) expecting to experience incivility in the next 24 hours[2], or the fact that only 18% of people polled trust leaders to tell the truth[3], the warning signs are all around us. Whether it's heated social media exchanges, tantrums at sporting events, leaders shirking responsibility, a lack of restraint in shared public places, discrimination, racism, or terrorism...and the list goes on and on, incivility is all around us. Our world is in dire need of positive, civil people treatment, that lifts others up.

The Golden Rule Civility Global Initiative aims to do this. Through strategic and consistent interruption, change-makers with both a mission to live The Golden Rule and the civility skill-set to be the change they want to see in the world, are making a difference. The end-in-mind is a world-wide culture of honor. For more than 20 years Lew Bayer and the team at Civility Experts Inc. have been working to gather the research, assess the current situation, start the conversation and to devise the tools, techniques, strategies, and skills matrix that will enable those who are already committed to the cause by their values choices, to behave, teach and lead though their skills – this ensures measurable outcomes.

The time for talking about a civility solution has run out. Most of us know what is right and wrong, and most of us believe in treating others with respect and kindness, we just don't know how to go about doing these things. It's time to build competency

---

[1] http://www.webershandwick.com/news/article/civility-in-america-2013-incivility-has-reached-crisis-levels

[2] https://www.webershandwick.com/uploads/news/files/Civility_in_America_2013_Exec_Summary. pdf

[3] https://www.forbes.com/forbes/welcome/?toURL=https://www.forbes.com/sites/tykiisel/2013/01/30/82-percent-of-people-dont-trust-the-boss-to-tell-the-truth/&refURL=https://www.google.ca/&referrer=https://www.google.ca/

in the skills that underpin the ability to exhibit civility so that we can take action. Now is the time!

Stated simply, The Golden Rule Civility Global Initiative challenges each of us to ask ourselves the Golden Rule Question, *'If I were receiving this same treatment, would I be okay with it?'*

This question applies to each of us, as we all contribute to the current situation in some positive and/or negative way whether we are cognizant of this contribution or not. When we take action in our personal relationships, homes, communities, churches, schools, political arenas, sports facilities, volunteer organizations, online, or in our workplaces...in each of these contexts we need to actively and consciously consider the implications and consequences of our actions. And then we need to be accountable for those outcomes.

Whether we perceive ourselves as in control, or as victims, there is no escaping the backdoor of people mistreatment. There are both short, and long-term consequences. The mistreatment of people- dehumanization- in whatever form it takes, will eventually come back upon us, and generations will continue to suffer. The ONLY way forward is respect, kindness, and civility. The ONLY way forward is to build cultures of honor where "human-kind" is the default approach, and where equality and honor are the desired outcomes. This is the ONLY way forward.

The collective teams at ICN and Civility Experts Inc., along with their colleagues at the International Civility Trainers' Consortium and The National Civility Center, continue to dedicate themselves to this great, and growing, global movement - The Golden Rule Civility Initiative.

The Golden Rule Civility Formula

We invite you to join us on the path. We can each make a difference.

Choose to adopt The Golden Rule philosophy of treating others the way you want to be treated as one of your personal values.

Choose to actively build your knowledge and skills so that you can exhibit civility every day. Building global cultures of honor is the only way forward.

How to Use This Book

Throughout the book you will see the Golden Rule Civility Initiative Icons. Civility starts with each of us. Each of us must commit to adopting The Golden Rule Philosophy in our own life. We must strive to ask ourselves the Golden Rule Question out of habit when we are interacting with others and making decisions about how we want to live and "be" in the world. And we must consciously make decisions about how to act in a civil manner. This requires conscious effort and continuous learning. We encourage you to pause at the various sections in the book, stop, think, ask yourself questions, search your history, and your heart for the answers, and then set personal goals for how you will move forward. Thank you for choosing Golden Rule

The "idea" icon, highlights a concept, or idea that is fundamental to Golden Rule Civility. These points are important to remember. If you are studying to be a Golden Rule Civility Statesman, these concepts should go in your study notes for when you prepare to take your certification exam.

The "ruler" is a measuring stick for tracking your behavior. When you see the ruler icon, a "change challenge" is presented. Make notes about what changes you will commit to making as you choose civility and live by the Golden Rule.

The "human-kind" icon represents YOU. When you see this icon, you are asked to reflect on your own thoughts, ideas, hopes, and values. Make notes about the change you want to see in the world. Write down books, or links or ideas, quotes, inspiration, prayers, etc.

The "crown of honor" icon highlights individuals or organizations who are examples of civility in action. Through their choices, words or actions, these are change-makers who are contributing positively and building cultures of honor.

Key Concept 1: The Golden Rule

"Treat others how you would want to be treated"

For centuries, people of various religions have endorsed a version of this life philosophy, which provides a basic approach on how to interact with others. As such, The Golden Rule cannot be claimed for any one philosophy, individual, or religion. Throughout history, many individual thinkers and spiritual traditions have promoted one or another version of The Golden Rule. And throughout history, the successful evolution of communities and countries has depended on its use as a standard through which conflict can be resolved.

In her book, *Think Humanism*, in a chapter about The Golden Rule, Maria MacLauchlan talks about how Humanists, and others, try to embrace the moral principle known as the 'Golden Rule', otherwise known as the ethic of reciprocity, which means we believe that people should aim to treat each other as they would like to be treated themselves – with tolerance, consideration, and compassion. This idea of The Golden Rule is what most people understand or think about when they hear the term.

Here are some additional examples of the different ways The Golden Rule has been expressed:

- Do not to your neighbour what you would take ill from him. (Pittacus, 650 BCE)

- Do not unto another that you would not have him do unto you. Thou needest this law alone. It is the foundation of all the rest. (Confucius, 500 BCE)

- Avoid doing what you would blame others for doing. (Thales, 464 BCE)

- What you wish your neighbors to be to you, such be also to them. (Sextus the Pythagorean,406 BCE)

- We should conduct ourselves toward others as we would have them act toward us. (Aristotle, 384 BCE)

- Cherish reciprocal benevolence, which will make you as anxious for another's welfare as your own. (Aristippus of Cyrene, 365 BCE)

- Act toward others as you desire them to act toward you. (Isocrates, 338 BCE)

- This is the sum of duty: Do naught unto others which would cause you pain if done to you. (From the ahabharata (5:1517), 300 BCE)

- What is hateful to you, do not to your fellow men. That is the entire Law; all the rest is commentary. (Rabbi Hillel 50 BCE)

- Thou shalt love thy neighbour as thyself. (From the

Christian Bible, Leviticus 19:18 1440 BCE)

- Therefore, all things whatsoever ye would that men should do to you, do ye even so to them. (Jesus of Nazareth, circa 30 CE)[4]

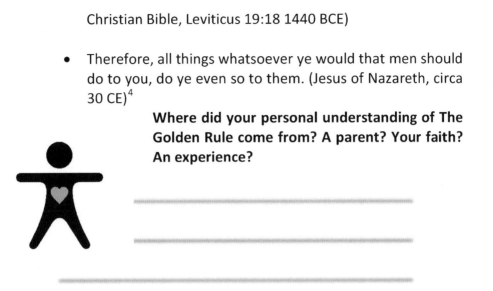

Where did your personal understanding of The Golden Rule come from? A parent? Your faith? An experience?

The Golden Rule doesn't really mean that you should treat someone else exactly as you'd want them to treat you ... it means that you should try to imagine how the other person might want to be treated, and then do that.

So, how do YOU want to be treated?

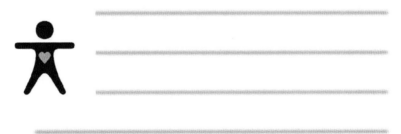

---

[4] From: http://www.thinkhumanism.com/the-golden-rule.html by Maria MacLauchlan 2007

Take a moment to think about this. What is important to you? For example, do you want respect? Kindness? Empathy? How often do you stop when you are engaging with someone and think about how you would feel if you were the other person- if you wouldn't like to be treated the way you are treating someone else, you need to stop what you are doing and change how you treat that person. When you are deliberate in trying to see the perspective of others and/or experience what someone else might be experiencing, it changes your attitude, demeanor, intention, and approach.

 Mark an X on the line indicating how often you stop and think about others before you speak or take action.

Rarely   Sometimes   Often   Most of the Time   Always

|--|

If you didn't put an "X" by "always", why not? What are the reasons why you don't always think of other before you take action? Write your thoughts here:

1.

2.

3.

4.

If you were assessing the extent to which you feel most people stop and think about you before they speak or interact with you, where would you mark them on the scale?

Rarely   Sometimes   Often   Most of the Time   Always

|--|

John F. Kennedy used the Golden Rule strategy of trying to see the perspective of others side during the controversial days of desegregation in the 1960s. Kennedy asked white Americans to imagine being looked down upon and treated badly based only on the color of their skin. He asked them to imagine how they would want to be treated if they were in that situation, and he encouraged them to act accordingly towards the black community.[5]

The Golden Rule and Social Grace

While the Golden Rule is a general, all-encompassing guideline for how to treat others, various cultures, communities, and societies also devise social rules and set expectations for interacting with each other in specific situations. These social rules are often understood as "etiquette" and following the rules is often understood to be an exhibition of social grace.

Unfortunately, one of the reasons people don't always exhibit The Golden Rule is because they are used to simply following social rules. Simply relying on the rules for direction can be problematic. For example, if you are just doing what a book or website or "expert" tells you to do, without thinking about who you are interacting with and considering the situation and conditions

---

[5] (From: "18 Practical Tips for Living the Golden Rule" by Leo Babauta), https://zenhabits.net/18-practical-tips-for-living-the-golden-rule/

around you, you could potentially do more harm than good.

Following along often leads to people simply not being in the habit of considering why they are doing what they are doing, or what the impact is of what they are doing. Generally, people make assumptions that the social rules they are following make their behavior "good enough" or they think they are doing the right thing just because that's the way things have always been done.

Whether we are talking about a table-setting or a handshake, the rules and rituals of etiquette have long held value. As early as 2500 B.C. with the first known manners guide, *The Instructions of Ptahhotep*, people have understood the technical aspects of courtesy. Choosing to follow the rules for dining, for entertaining, and for interacting with others, both socially and in business, has always been a necessary element of social polish. And there are aspects of etiquette evident in almost every culture around the world.

"Manners make it easier to live and work together. However, even though there may be no negative impact caused by being polite just out of habit, exhibiting manners just for the sake of being polite is not really all that civilized".

– Lew Bayer, CEO, Civility Experts Inc.

Following prescribed social conventions out of some sense of obligation, or being courteous just because you are directed to do so by some person or circumstance, without some measure of understanding and good intentions, is not nearly the same as choosing and practicing civility.

Think about behaviors you exhibit out of habit because it was your family tradition to do so, or because you have been instructed to do so. Do you know the rationale for these behaviors? Why do you exhibit them?

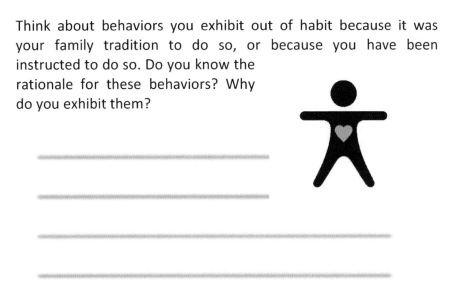

_____

_____

_____

_____

An important recognition when you choose civility and live by The Golden Rule is that well-intentioned gestures, and even unintended discourtesies can cause harm. This is why it is necessary to always consider the impact of our actions and to consider how the other person- the recipient of our words or actions - might feel, think, or act, as a result of those actions.

When you add conscious and deliberate behaviors such as non-judgment, respect for others, cultural consideration, adaptations to social style, consideration for the big picture, and a commitment to continually learn and change, you are better able to "show" your Golden Rule values. Each of these aspects of behavior are elements of civility.

Stated simply, The Golden Rule is an approach, a mentality or an attitude, and civility is a conscious and consistent choice to behave in a way that supports a Golden Rule attitude. Together you get Golden Rule Civility.

THE GOLDEN RULE SELF-ASSESSMENT

 Are You a Respectful Person?[6]
(Take this self-evaluation and decide for yourself.)

True	False	
☐	☐	I treat other people the way I want to be treated.
☐	☐	I am considerate of other people.
☐	☐	I treat people with civility, courtesy, and dignity.
☐	☐	I accept personal differences.
☐	☐	I work to solve problems without violence.
☐	☐	I never intentionally ridicule, embarrass, or hurt others.

---

[6] http://www.goodcharacter.com/ISOC/Respect.htmlde. Together you get Golden Rule Civility.

What are some other reasons you believe yourself to be a respectful person?

_____

_____

_____

_____

Vera Tembo Chiluba - Former First Lady of Zambia. She continues to be a strong voice to the people of Zambia. She is known for her care for the people of Zambia of all ages. She honors the lives of all Zambians and her love for her people is evident in her actions.

As you were completing the short self-assessment, did you notice the word respect? What is "respect" to you? Consider the power of words, for example, do you think everyone understands "respect" the same way you do?

_____

_____

_____

_____

What is Respect?

Being clear of what you mean when you say "respect" is very important. There is tremendous power in words. For example, for many people respect is understood to be something you have to earn. We often hear people say, "He/she has to earn my respect." Right? However, for most people, when we say, "He/she doesn't respect me," we are saying that based on the way someone is treating us, we don't feel valued. But how can we earn "value"?

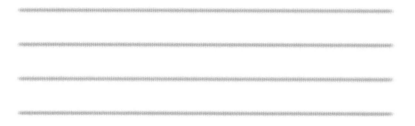

From a civility point of view, each of us has value. Each of us has equal value as a human being. Each of us has gifts and contributions to make. These are not things that we need to prove or have evaluated by another equal human being. As such we are all deserving of respect. Respect is something we should each have automatically given to us, just because we are human beings.

What are your thoughts on this? Do you believe each human being has equal value?

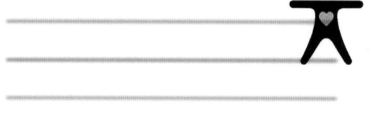

22

Why do you think more people don't practice The Golden Rule? Do you think it could have something to do with people not seeing the value in others?

_____

_____

_____

_____

 What did you take away from the section about The Golden Rule? Make a note of ideas, and concepts you'd like to remember. Write a goal statement about one thing you are going to do, or learn, or change personally in order to live by the Golden Rule.

_____

_____

_____

_____

KEY CONCEPT 2: CIVILITY

"Civility is its own reward" – Lew Bayer

If you are a change-maker you quickly come to understand that simply talking about human rights, equality, peace, and/or justice is just not enough. To be a change-maker you have to actually DO something. In this same way, it isn't enough just to talk about The Golden Rule. For example, telling people to treat others the way they want to be treated is a nice idea. But in and of itself, the idea of The Golden Rule is just an idea, a philosophy, a concept, a value...it's just talk, until you do something with it.

As such, to facilitate change related to how people treat each other, starting a conversation about positive people treatment is a necessary first step. But then, it's important to assess whether people have the skills they need to do the things they want to do. Change isn't always easy. And getting people to change what they believe can be very difficult. Doing these things – changing how people think and act requires a very specific skill set. This is where civility comes in. It is almost impossible to talk about The Golden Rule without also talking about civility.

When you live by The Golden Rule, the way you act, the way you talk, the way you make decisions, and the way you interact with people reflects your attitudes and values. These positive, respectful behaviors that convey a Golden Rule Philosophy is one way to describe what civility is. When you make conscious decisions to take specific actions in order to apply what you think about people treatment to how you are, how you think, how you talk, how you act, and how you treat others. When you do this, you are choosing and exhibiting civility.

So, what is "Civility" to you?
Write your thoughts here.

_____

_____

_____

_____

But Isn't Civility Just About Manners and Being Nice?

Just as many people confuse The Golden Rule with social grace, most people think civility is the same as etiquette or they understand it as a general concept, such as "manners", "respect" or "kindness". Is this what you think?

If so, you are only partly right. Etiquette comes from the French word meaning "ticket". It is thought that rules of etiquette began in the French Royal Court, which was made up of aristocrats with little else to do. They began to devise special rules that must be followed in the court which must eventually have become known as your "ticket" to royalty. The rules began to spread to other countries until they became widespread. In fact, up until the mid-1900's, students were taught manners and etiquette in school.

Regarding rules of etiquette, it is very important that people do understand a society's (or an organization's) rules for behavior. When you follow the social rules for a situation, you are perceived to have manners. When we know what to expect from others, and when we have standards in common, it is easier to be in relationship with people – at work or at home. Once we agree on the general rules, we can focus on what we are working towards together, versus continually sorting out individual actions and managing differing expectations. Having general rules for a context also helps us each set aside our personal opinions about what is considered polite, or respectful. If we take opinion out and everyone adheres to what the rules are for the context, this can eliminate potential miscommunications and/or judgments.

Defining Civility

There are a range of dictionary definitions for civility—most of these refer to the obvious connection between manners and etiquette and courtesy. However, these simple definitions do not accurately capture the attitudinal and values component so important to the practical applications of civility. The following expanded definition of civility, devised by the team at Civility Experts Inc. after 20 years in the field, helps to capture those complexities.

 That each of us understands that being civil is expected, and is often an unwritten rule, is very important. However, Civility Experts Inc. suggests that civility is about much more than just rules or manners. Civility is....

*A **conscious awareness** of the impact of one's thoughts, actions, words and intentions on others; combined with...*

*A **continuous acknowledgement** of one's responsibility to ease the experience of others (for example, through restraint, kindness, non-judgment, respect, and courtesy); and ...*

*A **consistent effort** to adopt and exhibit civil behavior as a non-negotiable point of one's character.* - Lew Bayer, CEO Civility Experts Inc.

For further clarification, one general way of distinguishing between the two concepts is to understand that etiquette guidelines, which incorporate manners, represent the rules or conventions that apply to a situation, a time, a culture, or a country.

Civility represents how the overriding values and character of an individual/community/organization/culture impact behavior and choices.

Does this definition of civility resonate with you? If so, why? If not, why not?

ETIQUETTE = CONVENTION (e.g., social rules)
GOLDEN RULE = CONSCIENCE (e.g., BELIEF in EQUAL VALUE + GIFTS = POSITIVE PEOPLE TREATMENT)

CIVILITY = CHOICES + BEHAVIOR (based on CONSCIOUS AWARENESS + CONTINUOUS ACKNOWLEDGEMENT + CONSISTENT EFFORT)

Think for a moment. Why do you think it is important to differentiate between etiquette and The Golden Rule and civility? Write your thoughts here.

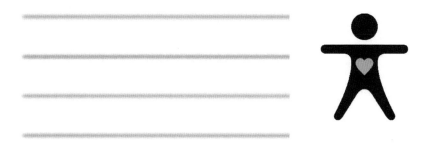

 Cedric Blackeagle - Former President and Chairman of the Crow Nation – He is a true humanitarian and peace maker for the Native American people of the United States, the Crow Nation. He has worked to keep water rights available for the people.

Where a person is, who and what he/she pays attention to can sometimes influence how he/she defines civility. Specifically, our experiences become a frame of reference. There are examples of different people defining civility in different ways all around you. For example, there has been a boom in "kindness" and "courage" programs, organizations and initiatives. And some people define civility as "peace". We are even seeing civility references in advertising, for example the Hilton Hotel chain references civility in their slogan.

Take some time to review the news and think about current events and individuals or communities in the global spotlight. Make a list of anyone you feel is identifying and/or defining civility in his/her specific context or organization.

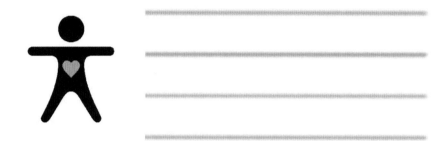

Remember to consider the acts and behaviors you see and don't always focus on the words because civility is often called different things.

Examples of civility in the news.

Sometimes it's easier to define civility if you have a sense of what civility "looks" like. Dr. Pier Forni, considered one of the foremost experts on civility suggests that there are at least 25 behaviors that  a person who is civil, actively engages in. Rate yourself on these behaviors.

Civility Self-Assessment

Adapted from 25 rules for civility by P.M. Forni

	Never	Sometimes	Frequently	Always
Pay Attention				
Acknowledge Others				
Think the Best				
Listen				
Be Inclusive				
Speak Kindly				
Don't Speak Ill				
Accept and Give Praise				
Respect Even a Subtle 'No.'				
Respect Others' Opinions				
Mind your Body				
Be Agreeable				
Rediscover Silence				
Respect Other				

People's Time				
Respect Other People's Space				
Apologize Earnestly				
Assert Yourself				
Avoid Personal Questions				
Care for your Guests				
Be a Considerate Guest				
Think Twice Before Asking for Favors				
Refrain from Idle Complaints				
Accept and Give Constructive Criticism				
Respect the Environment and be Gentle to Animals				
Don't Shift Responsibility and Blame				

Choosing Civility – More Than Just Being Kind and Following the Social Rules[7]

Choosing civility means that in expressing manners, you do so with purpose and have an understanding of the value of the rules beyond mere social requirements. For example, having the whole family sit at the table for dinner is not so much about acting civilized as it is about choosing to take time to be together, to laugh, to tell stories, to connect in some small way. Inviting guests over and making them feel welcome is a way of opening your heart, not just your front door. It's a way of letting people know that you are interested in sharing with them—food, the comforts of home, and maybe some conversation. Looking someone in the eye and extending a handshake tells that person that you choose to take a minute out of your busy, tired, stressful day to show another human being that he or she has value.

In addition to making value-based choices on purpose, conscious awareness is an important aspect of choosing civility.

You have to pay attention to the impact your choices, words, actions, and even lack of actions, have on others. It means using your social radar to assess the needs of others and building your social competence to accommodate those needs. You need to be able to interpret verbal and nonverbal cues, to adapt your behavior based on appropriateness in specific contexts.

Choosing civility means having the courage to consider how your actions impact others, and to do the right thing, even when your own physical or emotional comfort is at stake.

Choosing civility requires taking responsibility for the experience

---

[7] This segment from The Power of One, Lew Bayer, excerpt from The Power of Civility, Thrive Publishing.

of others and acknowledging that everyone deserves respect. You have a responsibility to be civil and kind to everyone, regardless of any benefit to yourself and regardless of whether you have a relationship or the same values as another person.

Choosing civility means having the courage to, or energy required to, be civil. Civility is its own reward[8]. When you extend respect and courtesy just because it is the right thing to do, when you exercise non-judgment, and when you relinquish any expectation of reciprocation for kindnesses you may offer, there is an authenticity and spirit of generosity, a graciousness that is expressed.

Civility itself exemplifies the elements required in creating a culture of honor[9]:

(Choosing) **civility** means having the courage to consider how your actions impact others, and the world as a whole and to do the right thing, even when your own physical or emotional comfort is at stake.

According to Dr. P. Forni, *"Beyond an attitude of benevolence to individuals, choosing civility entails an active interest in the well-being of our communities and even a concern for the health of the planet on which we live."* Choosing civility means having the courage to expend the time, money, or energy required to be civil. Civility is its own reward. When you extend respect and courtesy just because it is the right thing to do, when you exercise non-judgment, and when you relinquish any expectation of reciprocation for kindnesses you may offer, there is an authenticity and spirit of generosity, a graciousness that is

---

[8] Lew Bayer, Power of Civility, Thrive Publishing 2016

[9] The 30% Solution, Lew Bayer, 2016, Motivational Press

expressed. Choosing to give your time, resources, attention, well-wishes, love, kindness, and respect, with no expectation of return, has tremendous benefit to you as the giver as well as to the recipient. James D. Miles captures the notion of conveying kindness and respect as follows, *"You can easily judge the character of a man by how he treats those who can do nothing for him."*

There are approximately 20,000 seconds in each waking day. This means that on any given day you have up to 20,000 opportunities to choose civility.

It just takes one second to make a difference. With one choice, one word, one kind gesture, one moment of consideration, you can change someone's life. In one committed moment of courage you can show your true character. You have the power to create positive, lasting change simply by choosing civility.

What did you take from the section about The Golden Rule?

Make a note of ideas, and concepts you'd like to remember. And write a goal statement for one thing you are going to commit to learning or doing or changing.

KEY CONCEPT 3: GOLDEN RULE CIVILITY

Golden Rule Civility®

Golden Rule Civility is...Choosing to treat others humanely, and with care; accepting differences without judgment; being empathetic of the human condition; and, acknowledging each individual's unique gifts and equal value. – Golden Rule Civility Global Initiative

 As discussed in the first two sections of this book, the Golden Rule philosophy is the "WHAT", as in what we want to do. And civility is the "HOW", as in want to do.

Think about this for a minute. How often has someone said any of the following to you...?

- Show some respect
- Just be nice
- Don't judge
- Treat him/her how you'd like to be treated
- Be more empathetic

- Learn from your mistakes
- Be a better listener
- Be polite
- Speak kindly
- Give the benefit of the doubt

These statements support The Golden Rule. They capture the "what" we, (or your parent, or society, or the rule books) want you to do. However, the statements don't tell you "how" to do these things. Most people would agree that they want to be kinder or nicer or more polite. And they would like to share the perspective of others, but they just don't know how.

> *"No one is created to be a copy; each person has their individual DNA and value" – Dr. Donella Pitzl*

Civility, when you understand it to include conscious awareness, continuous acknowledgment, and consistent effort, is the answer to the question "how".

For example:

- Show some respect
  HOW? By treating people equally and acknowledging their value, avoid labels, build cultural competence so you learn social nuances that convey respect.

- Just be nice
  HOW? By choosing to say and do things that ease the experience of others.

- Don't judge
  HOW? By being consciously aware, e.g., by using your social radar, of the impact of judging, and/or by seeking to understand before passing judgment, and/or learn what is

at the root of someone's behavior.

- Treat him/her how you'd like to be treated
  HOW? By finding out how he/she might like to be treated, ask questions, study, watch... and don't assume he/she wants what you want.

- Be more empathetic
  HOW? Acknowledge that he/she is a living breathing human being with feelings and thoughts and dreams and wishes, experience and imagine what others are experiencing.

- Learn from your mistakes
  HOW? Respect yourself, find your value, search for your gift, accept that failing is learning and learning is growth, be a continuous learner.

Together, the Golden Rule philosophy combined with civility creates a comprehensive solution for all kinds of problems we are facing in the world today. Using Golden Rule strategies can help individuals, teams, organizations, communities, and entire countries.

When you combine The Golden Rule with Civility, you get *"Golden Rule Civility"*.

GOLDEN RULE CIVILITY includes, but is not limited to the following behaviors:

- choosing to treat others humanely and with care
- accepting differences without judgment
- being empathetic of the human condition, and
- acknowledging each individual's unique gifts and equal value.

The Golden Rule Civility Formula

GOLDEN RULE ATTITUDE + CIVILITY BEHAVIORS = HUMAN KIND + CULTURES OF HONOR

One of the benefits of Golden Rule Civility is "positive people treatment". The way individuals, leaders, communities, and even countries treat people, and how this treatment is expressed, has consequences. Negative people treatment has negative consequences. Even if you are not directly involved in the treatment, you can still be impacted by it indirectly. And when negative people treatment becomes a pattern, or part of the system, e.g., through our written and unwritten social rules, workplace codes of conduct, government legislation, etc. there is no avoiding the negative impact created.

People Treatment™

People Treatment is the way you approach, think about, speak to, and be with other people.   – Golden Rule Civility Global Initiative

Sometimes incivility is so well-ingrained in our daily experience that we grow accustomed to it and perceive it to be "normal". Incivility should never become normal. Review the chart below and check off behaviors that you have observed or experienced.

Think about your daily life. You can also consider your workplace and what you see happening in the media and in the public forum.

_____

_____

_____

_____

SYMPTOMS OF POOR PEOPLE TREATMENT AND INCIVILITY
By Civility Experts Inc. ©

❖ Persistent miscommunication, such as:

- o non-responsiveness
- o misunderstandings
- o arguments
- o withholding of information
- o diminished morale and/or mood
- o negative attitudes
- o lack of energy
- o poor engagement
- o lowered confidence
- o measurable lack of accountability

❖ Decreased productivity
❖ increased lateness
❖ Laziness
❖ Reduced quality and quantity of output
❖ Diminished collaborative effort
❖ Increased customer service complaints

- ❖ Visible decrease in product and/or service standards
- ❖ Growing gap in alignment between personal or corporate goals and leadership's abilities
- ❖ Lack of integrity and ethics
- ❖ Inability to adapt effectively to change
- ❖ Inability to navigate cultural and communication barriers
- ❖ Increased difficulty recruiting and hiring competent personnel
- ❖ Difficulty identifying and practicing core values
- ❖ Lowered common sense
- ❖ Failure to attend to social cues and follow social conventions
- ❖ Increased disengagement
- ❖ Difficulty maintaining relationships
- ❖ Less involvement in social, civic and community events

Throughout history there are countless examples of negative people treatment. One of the most horrific examples of negative people treatment was the ideologies and polices of Hitler during World War II. His hateful rhetoric and beliefs against people of the Jewish faith, homosexual individuals, individuals of ethnic backgrounds including Romanian, and Slavic peoples from Poland, Serbia, Ukraine and those of certain political background lead to the persecution and murder of millions of individuals.

Much of his policy and belief was focused on placing the blame for German losses during WWI and the resulting political and economic struggles and many ordinary individuals accepted this information and followed suit.

While this is an extreme example of negative people treatment it shows how easy it can be to be caught up in stereotypes and negative attitudes towards others.

A few additional examples of negative people treatment are:
- Genocide
- World wars

- Uncivil use of weapons
- Some immigration policies
- War
- Torture
- Discrimination

What are some other examples of events, changes, policies, people, etc., that have resulted in negative people treatment?

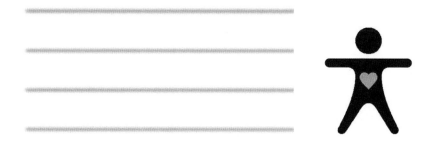

There are measurable costs and consequences of negative people treatment, a few examples:

- High cost of policing
- Fear
- Hatred
- Prejudice
- Fewer civil rights and liberties

We cannot escape the cost of poor people treatment. If we look at just one example, discrimination in the workplace, we can see tremendous impacts to individuals, to organizations, and even to industry sectors. Whether it be for sexual orientation, appearance, religious beliefs, family status, or ethnic or cultural background, this type of poor people treatment has an enormous cost. For the United States alone, research shows employers spend around $64 billion dollars a year replacing employees who leave jobs due to discrimination and unfair treatment. This is not a North American phenomenon either, gender discrimination is rampant in the Chinese job market, with women often not being considered or facing higher standards or requirements then men for the same job[10], thus shutting out an entire section of the population from fulfilling job needs, at an astronomical cost.

If we look more closely at workplace studies, the research shows that when there is incivility in the form of bias or inability to accept diversity, there are decreases in creativity. Performance and team spirit deteriorate, customers turn away, and companies bear large expenses in managing these incidents.[11]

When asked how incivility/poor people treatment impacts them personally at work, respondents said:
- 48% intentionally decreased their work effort
- 47% intentionally decreased the time spent at work
- 38% intentionally decreased the quality of their work
- 80% lost work time worrying about the incident
- 63% lost work time avoiding the offender
- 66% said that their performance declined
- 78% said that their commitment to the organization declined

[10] http://www.clb.org.hk/content/workplace-discrimination

[11] From: "Rude behavior at work is increasing and affects the bottom line" (January 30, 2013)

44

- 12% said that they left their job because of the uncivil treatment
- 25% admitted to taking their frustration out on customers[12]

The consequences of incivility and poor people treatment on a larger scale, for example when it impacts a whole country, can be significant and they are often immutable. As just one example, in South Africa when systematic racial segregation of the population, known as apartheid, allowed for the legal discrimination and horrible mistreatment of nonwhite South Africans.

The Cost and Consequences of People Treatment

All around the world, and since the beginning of time, people treatment has impacted us, e.g., wars that change the course of history, but each of us is also impacted daily by how we are treated. Now that you have acknowledged that you experience negative people treatment (incivility), let's take a closer look at how incivility impacts each of us.

Consider impacts such as:

- Physical
- Psychological
- Emotional
- Relational
- Social
- Economic
- Cultural

---

[12] Thunderbird School of Global Management
https://www.sciencedaily.com/releases/2013/01/130130184048.htm

How has incivility impacted you personally? E.g., have you experienced low self-esteem or panic attacks due to prolonged bullying?

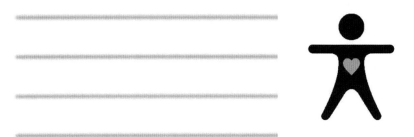

Have you changed how you interact with people as a result of constant incivility related to your age, gender or cultural background?

Do you know others who have been impacted by negative people treatment? If so, who? And how?

Consider how different contexts related to long-term incivility can impact us, for example:

- What happens when you are surrounded by people who experienced incivility, e.g., genocide, concentration camps, persecution?
- World events, e.g., acts of terrorism
- Policies, e.g., equal rights
- Political events, e.g., dictatorships
- Natural events e.g., catastrophes that whole communities never completely recover from
- Trends and social influences, e.g., social media
- Culture e.g., you live in a place where incivility such as war is a constant

Can you think of any specific contextual conditions that have impacted you long- term in a negative way?

It is important to note that sometimes, world events, changes, policies, people, etc., occur that have resulted in positive people treatment, for example:

- Human rights guidelines
- The United Nations
- Employment Equity policies
- Accommodation

- Martin Luther King
- Mother Theresa
- Ghandi
- Red Cross

Can you think of events, people, or changes in your personal experience that have resulted in positive people treatment?

_____

_____

_____

_____

Positive People Treatment Can Prevent a "Gift Famine"

If your focus is fostering positive people treatment, human-kindness, and building cultures of honor, it ALL starts with The Golden Rule. Dr. Clyde Rivers has been speaking and teaching on The Golden Rule for years and one of the consequences he highlights is the notion of a "gift famine" if/when incivility prevails.

Dr. Rivers asks us to remember that when we impact the emotions, physicality, and spirit of another person through incivility, we potentially eliminate the opportunity for that person to use his/her gifts. It may be that the little girl who is bullied such that she isn't confident, never finds the courage to raise her voice or share her intellect – and maybe she has as her gift a long-sought after solution to a well-known human problem. When we dishonor people, we take away their gift to the world. This is a serious consequence that we frequently don't consider.

As we honor people in any arena of life, the culture around us changes. The concept of honor is a key aspect of The Golden Rule Civility Global Initiative co-founded by the authors, Dr. Rivers and Dr. Bayer. The Golden Rule Philosophy at the root of our attitudes and choices, and civility- specifically having the skills that enable us to exhibit civility consistently and effectively is another key piece to building cultures of honor. You need both the attitude (Golden Rule Civility Philosophy) and the behavior/skills (Civility Competency) to be able to change how people think and act.

Senator Jim Beall – Senator Beall is a major player in helping bring better education to the youth and children of the State of California. He is a Golden Rule Intl. World Peace Ambassador appointed through iChange Nations™

What did you take away from the section about The Golden Rule? Make a note of ideas, and concepts you'd like to remember. Write a personal goal about something you are going to do, learn or change related to Golden Rule Civility.

_____

_____

_____

_____

KEY CONCEPT 4: COLLABORATION

Collaboration is...

Consciously and strategically working together towards achieving a shared goal, all while recognizing that the collective output is greater than any one individual's contribution.
– Golden Rule Global Civility Initiative

In a world where there is a lot of talk about how "We're all in this together", it's interesting that true collaboration seems in short supply. And at a time when resources are dwindling, and there are a myriad of big problems- some on a global scale, such as climate control/global warming, terrorism, threats of nuclear war, etc., collaboration is needed now more than ever.

While many of us have been on teams before and may consider ourselves team players, "team- orientation" doesn't necessarily mean we are effective collaborators.

What do you think is the difference between collaboration and teamwork?

_____

_____

_____

_____

What do you think?

Collaboration requires:

a)   shared purpose
b)   trust
c)   goals
d)   good people
e)   a, b, and c

See bottom of page for answer

Collaboration requires: Emotional engagement, trust, willingness to accept skills or talent of others as equal or better, ability to self-direct, AND, most important, collaborators accept a shared purpose that may or may not benefit all involved equally.

Teamwork requires: Completing tasks together, however, each team member doesn't necessarily contribute equally. And you don't have to agree with the team goals or end-in-mind to be on the team or to make a contribution. In addition, typically when a team "wins" the whole team is credited with the win, and they all benefit equally, regardless of their contributions.

e)   is the correct answer.

Can you think of a time you were collaborating versus just being on a team?

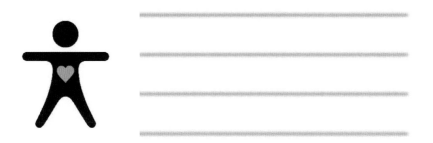

Because collaborators accept a shared purpose that may or may not benefit all involved equally, an essential ingredient to successful collaboration is generosity. Generosity of spirit, of goodwill and of kindness. This generosity is one aspect of what makes "good" people (referencing (d) in the What do you think? question above).

But generosity in the context of Golden Rule Civility is not just about being kind and giving. It's about HOW you give. Specifically, you need to give with no expectation of return. One term related to this idea is "human-kind".

Human-kind®
Being human-kind means doing what will ease the experience of others simply because you choose love, and your humanness compels you to do so. – Lew Bayer, CEO Civility Experts Inc.

As you venture down the path of civility, you will inevitably encounter those who do not receive your gifts graciously. It is sometimes difficult to accept and understand why some people choose incivility even when they are being presented with kindness and love. There are many reasons for this, and some of the strategies for addressing these difficult situations is covered in The Golden Rule Civility Statesman training. However, one way or another, forgiveness is at the root of each strategy. At some point you have to find a way to forgive incivility and move forward.

After years working in the field of civility, Lew Bayer, CEO of Civility Experts Inc. has observed that the attribute that enables people to forgive others when acts of civility are not reciprocated is "human-kindness". Human-kindness is an innate goodness that could be described as hope, faith, or believe in the good in people. When we are human-kind, we understand and are empathetic to the human condition. We acknowledge that each of us has his/her own struggles- some known, some unknown, and we are each doing the best we can do with the knowledge and tools, supports and strengths that we have to work with.

It is human-kindness, that enables forgiveness. And it is human-kindness that enables us to give to others with no expectation of return. Baring any physical or emotional barriers, the capacity to be human-kind resides in us all.

Golden Rule Civility also requires **nonjudgment**. We do not know what it is like to be another person. We haven't experienced the same personal history, life experiences, family, geographic, genetic or cultural conditions, and we don't know all the and unique characteristics of a person or the experiences that are specific to him/her.

Each human being is a package of completely unique perceptions and experiences. We do not have access to all that made them who they are. For that reason, we never have enough information to judge a person. So instead of assuming a person is doing something 'inappropriate" because he/she mean harm, why not assume that person is doing the best he/she can according to what he/she knows and the resources available to him/her?

And if you do make assumptions, why not assume the best? This is called "giving the benefit of the doubt".[13]

Can you think of a time when you made an assumption about a person, and realized later you had made a mistake?

_____

_____

_____

_____

Has someone ever made incorrect assumptions about you? How did that make you feel?

_____

_____

_____

_____

[13] From Social IQ: Bringing Civility Back to the Workplace, 2011, Lew Bayer, Columbia Books

Can you recall an act of "human-kindness" – that is when someone was particularly kind or sympathetic to you/your situation?

When people are "human-kind" they are focused on positive people treatment and so not always concerned about what they personally are going to take-away from a situation. This enables effective collaboration. Having said all this, good intentions are not always enough. In addition to positive intent and positive attitude. It is necessary for collaborators to be skilled at communication, negotiation, presenting themselves positively, building trust etc. These skills are all skills that support an ability to exhibit civility. In the Golden Rule Civility Statesman Certification course, all of these required skills are addressed.

To have a clearer understanding of why collaboration is not always a simple endeavor, take some time to review the Collaboration Pyramid. You can see how collaboration is a process and how there are foundational pieces that have to be in place in order to achieve superior results.

Collaboration for Superior Results

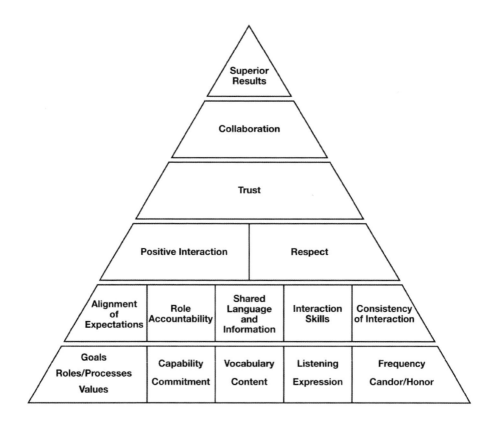

nFusion Model for Effective Collaboration[14]

_____

[14] http://nfusion.com/blog/thought-leadership-building-culture-collaboration/

Background on the Collaboration Behind Creation of The Golden Rule Civility Global Initiative

 The Community Civility Counts campaign was launched in the spring of 2015 as a joint partnership between the Gary Chamber of Commerce and The Times Media Co. Hughes credits Gordon E. Bradshaw, the chamber's public policy chairman, for bringing the idea forward at a March 2015 committee meeting and for designing a poster.

That poster caught the attention of Rivers of the Golden Rule International and president and founder of iChange Nations™

Hughes said the Community Civility Counts was born "after observing so many acts of incivility and cruel behavior ... On behalf of the Gary Chamber, our board of directors and members, I want to extend a special gesture of gratitude to our civility partners from around the country and all of you who have traveled near and far to promote kindness and consideration toward your fellow man."

He also saluted a troupe of young people from the South Shore Dance Alliances who entertained in African costumes to the beat of African drums, a performance that drew sustained applause. "We are celebrating the nations today," Bradshaw said in his invocation, citing the need for kindness and civility "in a world of indifference."

During his keynote address, Indiana Attorney General Curtis Hill said civility is a necessity if "America is going to lead the world." Hill said he grew up during Ronald Reagan's presidency. "Ronald Reagan actually had a cordial relationship with (Speaker of the

House) Tip O'Neill. They were able to work together on programs that helped the nation," Hill said. "I remember one of Reagan's comments – 'I'd rather have half a loaf than none at all'."

Civility, he said, needs to begin locally, within families and communities. "We need to love thy neighbor, turn the other cheek," Hill said. "But remember we only have two cheeks."

Community Civility Counts has grown from a local initiative to treat others with respect into an international movement that continues to earn kudos.

"We could not have predicted, even last April (2015) when Community Civility Counts' first World Civility Day sold out at the Majestic Star Casino in Gary, that we would have a full day of outstanding workshops and an even bigger and better gala dinner in year two," said Bob Heisse, editor of The Times Media Co.

In recent months, The Times Media Co. has also won the Associated Press Media Editors' Innovator of the Year Award and a Lee Enterprises' President's Award for the Community Civility Counts initiative.

In an Editor & Publisher article about The Times, the writers specifically cited 2016 as beginning "with a high point for the initiative when the Indiana Senate unanimously approved a resolution commending the group 'for delivering an awareness campaign to remind everyone about the need for civility and treating each other right'." That resolution was authored by Sen. Lonnie Randolph, D-East Chicago, and supported by all 50 Senate members from both political parties.

59

The following week, the Indiana House of Representatives approved the same resolution authored by Rep. Vernon Smith, D-Gary.

Dr. Clyde Rivers and Lew Bayer met at World Civility Day in April 2017. Dr. Rivers has taken on the role of Spokesman for the event and Lew was presenting a workshop on Civility in the Workplace. It was on that occasion that the two recognized that their paths were meant to cross. Each was successful in his/her own way, however, they realized that together- by marrying The Golden Rule, which was Dr. Rivers' focus, and Civility Skill Building, which was Lew's focus, they could collaborate and facilitate a global movement towards building cultures of honor.

Dr. Clyde Rivers, is a highly sought-after voice for peace around the world. His message of the Golden Rule, "Treat other the way you want to be treated," has qualified him for some of the world's most prestigious recognition.

Dr. Rivers is the winner of the first Congressional Danny K. Davis Peace Prize Award 2017. He was recognized as one of the top collaborators in America with an Honorable Mention for the American Civic Collaboration Award 2017. https://www.civvys.org/

Dr. Clyde Rivers is the Spokesman for Community Civility Counts, World Civility Day. Dr. Rivers is also the North America Representative for Interfaith Peace-Building Initiative to the United, and the Voice of the Golden Rule. www.uri.org

Dr. Rivers is the Founder and President of iChange Nations™ Inc, an organization dedicated to developing a culture of honor around the world, giving iChange Nations™ Inc the title of the "Largest network creating cultures of honor around the world." His organization is training statesman to have the knowledge of how to bridge the span into the policy making rooms of the world to make a difference. As the Golden Rule Dialogue Expert, Dr. Rivers works tirelessly to create dialogue where people can work out their differences to move forward in the peace-making process. http:// ichangenations.org/

Lew believes that "Civility is its own reward". She suggests that "In choosing civility, people find their best self, and in doing so, they experience the grace, courage, generosity, humanity, and humility that civility engenders."

For almost 20 years Lew Bayer has been internationally recognized as a leading civility expert. With a focus on social intelligence and culturally-competent communication, the team at Civility Experts – which includes 176 affiliates in 35 countries has supported 100's of organizations in building better workplaces. In addition to her role as CEO of multinational civility training group Civility Experts Inc. www.CivilityExperts.com , Lew is Chair of the International Civility Trainers' Consortium, volunteer Director of the National Civility Center, www.civilitycenter.org and she is also a proud mentor for The Etiquette House, a member of the Advisory Board for A Civil Tongue, President of The Center for Organizational Cultural Competence www.culturalcompetence.ca, and Founder of the In Good Company Etiquette Academy Franchise Group www.ingoodcompanyetiquette.com. In early 2017, Lew co-founded the Golden Rule Civility Global Initiative with Dr. Clyde Rivers. Lew received an honorable mention for a Civvy Collaboration award in 2017, an AICI Award recognizing her as a Civility Change-Maker, an honorary doctorate in Ethics and Social Justice, a Civility Counts Award at World Civility Day in 2016, and several prestigious awards from ICN for her work in global civility including an honorary doctorate in Ethics and Social Justice.

Vanda Pignato - Former 1st Lady of El Salvador. She has worked tirelessly protecting women's rights in the country of El Salvador. She is a recipient of the iChange Nations™ Global Leadership Award.

Golden Rule Civility Initiatives and Collaboration can happen at a range of levels, e.g., at the individual level where men and women work to build civility in their homes. At the community level, organizational level, government level, and at a global level. One of the goals of The Golden Rule Civility Global Initiative is to train Golden Rule Civility Statemen to help build cultures of honor all over the world.

Real-life Example of Successful Community Collaboration:[15]

 Medicine Hat, a city in southern Alberta, Canada, pledged in 2009 to put an end to homelessness. Now they say they've fulfilled their promise.

No one in the city spends more than 10 days in an emergency shelter or on the streets. If you've got no place to go, they'll simply provide you with housing. "We're pretty much able to meet that standard today. Even quicker sometimes," Mayor Ted Clugston tells, "As It Happens" host, Carol Off.

Housing is tight in Medicine Hat. Frequent flooding in the past few years didn't help matters. With money chipped in by the province, the city built many new homes.

Ted Clugston is the mayor of Medicine Hat, Alberta. Clugston admits that when the project began in 2009, when he was an alderman, he was an active opponent of the plan. "I even said some dumb things like, 'Why should they have granite countertops when I don't,'" he says. "However, I've come around to realize that this makes financial sense."

Clugston says that it costs about $20,000 a year to house someone. If they're on the street, it can cost up to $100,000 a year. "This is the cheapest and the most humane way to treat people," he says.

"Housing First puts everything on its head. It used to be, 'You want a home, get off the drugs or deal with your mental health

---

[15] 15 http://www.cbc.ca/radio/asithappens/as-it-happens-thursday-edition-1.3074402/medicine-hat-becomes-the-first-city-in- canada-to-eliminate-homelessness-1.3074742

issues,'" Clugston says. "If you're addicted to drugs, it's going to be pretty hard to get off them, if you're sleeping under a park bench."

And the strategy has worked. In Medicine Hat, emergency room visits and interactions with police have dropped. But there was one change that initially surprised Clugston — court appearances went up. "They end up dealing with their past, atoning for their sins," he says.

Clugston believes that no one on the streets is unreachable. He says city staff found housing for one man, but he insisted on leaving to sleep under cars. Day after day, they'd search him out and take him back to his new home.

"They did it 75 times, but they had the patience and they didn't give up on him and, eventually, he ended up staying in the house," he says. "Ultimately, people do want a roof over their heads."

The inevitable step in building an effective team is for each member of the team to get to know each other – but not only by their names. The thing is to get to know somebody's values, goals, strengths and the way they work. Once you know your teammates like that, it will be easier to define how to work together best. In their research, Harvard Business Review found that "the higher the proportion of strangers on the team and the greater the diversity of background and experience, the less likely the team members are to share knowledge or exhibit other collaborative behaviors."

What did you take away from the section about The Golden Rule? Make a note of ideas, and concepts you'd like to remember. Write down a goal statement for something you can commit to doing, learning or changing related to Golden Rule Civility.

_____

_____

_____

_____

"We can't solve problems with the same thinking used when we created them." - Einstein

KEY CONCEPT 5: END-IN-MIND-THINKING

End-in-mind Thinking
Refers to considering the ultimate and core objective when making decisions and problem- solving. When building Golden Rule Civility Culture, end-in-mind thinking incorporates a shared purpose to facilitate peace, honor, and civility.
– Golden Rule Civility Global Initiative

You may recall that the sub-title of this book is, "An action plan for building a culture of honor". The culture of honor part is the end-in-mind for the Golden Rule Civility Global Initiative. Building cultures of honor where the outcomes are that civility is the default action and where people treat each other according to the Golden Rule is the ultimate goal, and mission, of The Golden Rule Civility Global Initiative. When this **end- in-mind** outcome is achieved, our work is done. The process for successful Golden Rule Civility Initiatives consists of 5 steps:

STEP 1: Awareness Raising and Resource Gathering

This step includes active promotion of the Initiative through social media and other marketing and promotional avenues. In addition to celebrating people and cultures of honor, the Initiative also includes actively gathering data and details about ongoing civility-oriented activities. An ongoing compilation of individuals and organizations can be found at www.goldenrulecivility.com/Directory

STEP 2: Training

One of the most important pieces of the Golden Rule Civility Global Initiative is the Golden Rule Civility Statesman training. There are 8 core skills taught for Level 1 Statesman training and 4 additional skills taught at the Master Statesman level. In total, about 80 hours of training as well as practice, references, evidence of application of the learning, and a score of 85% or higher is required to achieve Golden Rule Civility Statesman status. Training is available live or online. There is also Golden Rule Civility Kids curriculum available. (for ages 5-8)

STEP 3: Assessing the Situation

The role of Golden Rule Civility Statesmen is to actively seek out situations, cultures, and contexts where incivility, disrespect, or dishonor are present. Statemen are taught how to assess change readiness and to co-devise change plans with stakeholders who are interested in building cultures of civility and honor.

STEP 4: Interrupting

Depending on the specific issue identified, and based on the timeline, resources and specific change goals, Golden Rule Civility Statesmen will deploy and engage in strategic "interruption strategies" to stop uncivil attitudes and behavior, and re-align individuals and groups towards building cultures of honor.

STEP 5: Supporting the Change

Civility change initiatives are not short-term solutions. Building cultures of honor takes time and commitment. Once the change has been initiated, the work and support - which may include resources, training, inspiration, coaching, mentorship, acknowledgment, etc., - continues.

Various dictionaries define an "outcome" as an observable end result, a consequence, a change in performance, something that follows from an action. It's also defined as a conclusion reached through the process of logical thinking. Change and logical thinking are both critical to the success of the Golden Rule Civility Global Initiative.

Let's start with change. Many people do not understand the complexities of change initiatives. This is evidenced by research showing that 70% of change initiatives fail.[16]

Somewhere along the way, the change management strategies and processes we've been using have become ineffective. 70% is a lot of failure. And a lot of time, a lot of resources, a lot of frustration, and surely results in a lot of bad behavior carried forward.

Over the last 20 years, the team at Civility Experts has worked predominately with workplaces who want to build a culture of civility in their organizations. Most of these workplace change initiatives were successful, but some were not. When the Civility Experts team started to compile their project findings and review the field research more closely, they began to understand what causes incivility in the workplace, and when they started to track the nature and frequency of uncivil behavior, some patterns began to emerge. Many of these patterns are well-ingrained behaviors and habits of mind. Further, many of these negative and/or uncivil patterns are actually endorsed through, and facilitated by, the organization's processes and procedures. In their work at the government level and in working with governments, the team at iChange Nations Inc was seeing some of

---

[16] As many as 70% of corporate and other organizational change efforts fail, according to research conducted by MC Associates, the change management and leadership development unit of Manchester Partners International.

these same patterns.

Expecting that we can change deep-set attitudes, thinking patterns, and behaviors just by putting up posters, or talking about the same problems over and over, is just not realistic. And to expect these "talk" remedies to result in positive change that takes hold quickly, and sticks ongoing contextual changes, doesn't seem at all reasonable. Yes, awareness raising is important but it's not nearly enough.

 First, we must understand and acknowledge that to take root, a civility change initiative must be strategic, well-planned, and long-term, and there has to be a clarified rationale for civility in the first place.

Making lasting, positive change takes time. Changing how people think and act takes time. Teaching the Golden Rule and civility skill-building takes time. Just like most change initiatives, building cultures of honor is going to take some time, money, and energy. You'll likely have to delegate people, and resources and you'll have to manage both the process and the people sides of the change. To be successful, you will have to have a plan that includes identifying stakeholders, assigning roles, completing assessments, setting goals, implementing the plan, delivering alignment communications, planning and delivering training, and evaluating. How complex and costly each of those components are will depend on the context and on your priorities. To be clear, when we talk about how complex a Golden Rule Civility initiative might be, we are referring to how many components are included in the plan. This is different from the level of difficulty or how complicated the initiative might be. Golden Rule Civility as a change initiative might be complex in that there are a lot of components to consider, but it isn't necessarily complicated.

Second, we must understand and acknowledge that the work will be ongoing and continuous. The reality is, due to the fact that the situation, the people, the priorities, and the conditions in a situation – whether a community, a workplace or a country – will change constantly.

As a result, you are never really finished with civility as a change initiative. Just to be clear… there is no end point. You are NEVER really finished with civility as a change initiative. And this is an extremely important realization. This realization is one of the biggest barriers most organizations face in moving forward with civility initiatives. Planning and implementation can be very hard work initially. It is going to cost some time and money and you have to be wholly committed long-term.

> Many individuals, teams, and organizations simply do not have the capacity- in terms of their skill set to make the required change. Skills-wise, the organization is not "change ready."
>
> - Lew Bayer

Can you think of a change initiative you were involved in that worked? If it worked, why did it work?

So, change readiness- the ability to anticipate and manage change is critical to the success of the Golden Rule Civility Global Initiative. Change readiness skills are one part of the comprehensive training Golden Rule Civility Statesmen will acquire as they prepare to engage in civility change initiatives. Another core skill that underpins the ability to be civil and to facilitate change is Systems Thinking.

 Systems Thinking [is] a way of thinking about, and a language for describing and understanding, the forces and interrelationships that shape the behavior of systems.

This discipline helps us to see how to change systems more effectively, and to act more in tune with the natural processes of the natural and economic world.[17]

With respect to Golden Rule Civility, change-makers and Golden Rule Civility Statesmen need to understand how all the pieces fit together. They need to know how each individual, each role, each condition and factor influences behavior and attitudes. They need to be able to see how one part of a system can impact the other positively or negatively.

---

[17] http://www.thwink.org/sustain/glossary/SystemsThinking.htm

Illustration: Fish Tank Metaphor[18]

We can liken an organization to a fish tank, with the Civility Statesmen (change-leaders) and general population as the fish. The system elements such as how many fish live in the tank, water condition, food, the tank itself, etc. become social and environmental influences on the fish.

The fish (people) need to navigate, swim and survive in these waters. The waters contain essential nutrients, but unless conditions are perfect, they are rarely pure, clear and favorable. In fact, they are often toxic and opaque, the cause of much confusion, unclear vision, and stress.

The waters contain unseen but strongly felt undercurrents in their shadows that are part of what surrounds everyone, including Civility Statesmen when they try to take a leadership role. The result is frequently a collapse of over-stressed individual fish, and in extreme circumstances the tank as a whole ('systemic failure').

In this murky environment Civility Statesmen are expected to exercise leadership. It is also their job to clean the tank. Unhelpfully, the toxins may come from above, though that's not the default Civility Statesmen assumption. Not able to see the tank for what it is, and not knowing how to set about cleaning their environment, some Statesman (leaders) flounder in the shallows and do what is easiest: they seek out the small fry. When not bearing down on them, they take them out, tell them to smarten up, make them look good with a little training, say if they're good they'll reward them with a bonus, and plop them back into the same murky water.

---

[18] http://www.systemicleadershipinstitute.org/systemic-leadership/theories/the-metaphor-of-the-fish-tank/

Some of the system elements have aspects that are as intended and designed; they comprise the legitimate or official system, e.g., maybe there is a water filter in the tank. Other aspects are unintended, including changes outside the tank (temperature, movement) and inside the tank (unwritten rules e.g., bigger fish get more food, politics, sickness, etc., these changes comprise the informal or shadow system.

Both the official/formal system and the unofficial/shadow system have positive and negative effects on the fish: both systems can be supportive, and/or both can make the 'water' toxic and inhibit the free exercise of honorable, transparent, and energetic leadership.

The system's combined effect on permitting or frustrating leadership is more powerful than any individual person's skills, behaviors or personality. All of which leads to the moral of this story: (as one book reviewer put it) "stop polishing the fish and tackle the water they swim in".[19]

Systemic means affecting most or all of a system rather than a small portion of the system. In medicine, systemic means affecting the entire body, rather than a single organ or body part. In systems thinking, systemic means arising from the structure of the system and affecting the general behavior of the entire system.

In social problems systemic means originating from the structure of the system in such a manner as to affect the behavior of most or all social agents of certain types, as opposed to originating from individual agents. In regard to civility and overall lack of the Golden Rule, we frequently reference "a civility crisis" which

---

[19] Adapted from: http://www.systemicleadershipinstitute.org/systemic-leadership/theories/the-metaphor-of-the-fish-tank/

indicates a systemic problem.

Can you think of an example or two of "systemic" problems you are aware of? Why is recognizing that incivility is systemic is important?

From the definition we see that a problem is systemic if the behavior of most or all of its important social agents is affected. The sustainability problem is clearly a systemic problem.

Systemic problems arise from the structure of the system. Since the sustainability problem is a systemic system, its solution requires deep systemic change to the fundamental layer of the system's structure. This differs radically from popular solutions, which because they don't go deep enough are superficial solutions.

The guiding principle is: Systemic problems require systemic solutions.

Systemic solutions resolve root causes. A systemic solution is the same thing as a root cause solution. Systemic solutions change the fundamental way a system works by changing the structure of its key feedback loops.[20]

---

[20] http://www.thwink.org/sustain/glossary/Systemic.htm

By their nature, celebrations and ceremonies of honor present a new structure for a feedback loop that represents one small way we can trigger change in a flawed, uncivil system.

"At its root, the cause of systemic incivility; dishonor, lack of human-kindness, racism, greed, etc., is a shift away from positive people treatment. We have allowed a self-serving focus to whittle away our humanity. We need to make conscious, and careful change to the way we think. Incivility at the levels we are currently experiencing it, is a deep-set, crisis of conscience and character"   – Lew Bayer

What did you take away from the section about The Golden Rule? Make a note of ideas, and concepts you'd like to remember.

KEY CONCEPT 6: CULTURE OF HONOR

Honor

To honor means to recognize the value of another and to acknowledge that each person is a gift from God, created to bring a contribution to the world. – Golden Rule Civility Global Initiative

For many years, Dr. Clyde Rivers and the team at iChange Nations Inc have been focused on the concept of honor. Dr. Rivers has been working with leaders of organizations, heads of state, and international leaders to initiate civil dialogue and change processes to build cultures of honor. Together with Civility Experts Inc. the organization is now training Golden Rule Civility Statesman to have the knowledge and skills to help move Golden Rule philosophy and civility behavior into the policy making rooms of the world. As the Golden Rule Dialogue Expert, Dr. Rivers works tirelessly to create opportunities for dialogue where people can work out their differences and move forward in the peacemaking process. http://ichangenations.org/

"You will never build a positive nation with a negative mindset"   - Dr. Clyde Rivers

iChange Nations Inc. is also building the world's largest honoring network by actively seeking out and acknowledging individuals, organizations and countries committed to, and contributing to, building cultures of honor.

"Golden Rule Civility Statesman award recipients are individuals who have displayed exemplary leadership to empower mankind. The mission of iChange Nations is to bring back the lost art of honor by building a culture that recognizes and honors these individuals throughout the world. iChange Nations Inc is a professional institution that equips, mentors, and trains highly esteemed individuals who have the desire to change nations throughout the world. Our candidates impact communities with trust and dignity, having improved the quality of life for those they have touched through their humanitarian leadership under the organizations and businesses in which they serve. Others have contributed towards the advancement of mankind through their ideology, inventions and leadership, which adds to already existing world knowledge".

– Dr. Donella Pitzl with iChange Nations Inc.

The end-in-mind for all Dr. Rivers' effort is to build Golden Rule Civility Cultures of Honor. Can you recall a time when you felt honored?

Golden Rule Culture of Civility and Honor

A new culture, where human-kind abounds, where honoring and valuing others is the expectation, and the norm. In a culture of civility and honor people treatment is based on The Golden Rule.
— Dr. Clyde Rivers

All around the world there is evidence that we are experiencing a crisis of conscience, of character, and of civility. We need a solution. Golden Rule Civility is the way forward. The mission of The Golden Rule Civility Global Initiative is to offer new ways of thinking, skill- building, and honoring, to move people all around the world towards building cultures of honor. Many, many individuals and organizations have been working in the field of civility and many others working in the area of The Golden Rule. You can learn more about these organizations by visiting the Civility Directory at www.goldenrulecivility.com.

Each of these organizations and individuals may be making some small strides forward but frequently individuals and/or organizations are focused on "What" (philosophy/attitude) e.g., kindness, ethics, diversity, etiquette, respect, peace, wellness, civility, justice, civil dialogue, etc., and doing an excellent job of awareness raising. Or, they are focused on the "How" (behavior) e.g., communicating better, using emotional intelligence, being culturally aware, practicing empathy, managing change, exhibiting social polish, etc., and they are doing a good job in these areas.

The Golden Rule Civility Global Initiative is the only initiative that combines both of these critical pieces: Attitude/Philosophy and Behavior/Skill. And this is why The Golden Rule Civility Global Initiative is having significant impact all around the world. It is collaboration and brining all the parties together that will result in a lasting solution.

The Golden Rule Civility Global Initiative consists of a well-thought out process for making long- lasting, sustainable change. There are five main steps to the process:

Step 1: Awareness Raising and Resource Gathering
Step 2: Assessing the Situation
Step 3: Training – Competency Based Civility Skills (8)
Step 4: Interrupting Incivility
Step 5: Supporting the Change

The Golden Rule Civility Initiative Change Cycle

Honor

There are four main conditions that must be met (pre-requisites) in order for the Golden Rule Civility Change Cycle to be effective. These are:

- Change Readiness (includes conscious recognition of the value of others)
- Acceptance of Golden Rule Civility as the way forward
- Honorable, skilled leadership with ability to interrupt incivility and lead change

Recognizing the Value of Others

Underpinning the "Culture of Honor" mindset and mission, that has been initiated by Dr. Clyde Rivers, is the belief that every person has value. Specifically, there is an unwavering belief that when each person is born, he/she has been endowed with a gift- or maybe multiple gifts. Those who endorse a culture of honor also recognize and believe that each of us has a moral obligation and a personal responsibility to do what we can to use our own gifts, but also to help and support, and lead others to using their gifts. Doing so is honoring ourselves and each other.

Most leaders understand that recognizing an individual, e.g., an employee in a workplace, a citizen in a community, who is making a positive contribution is motivating to the individual being recognized as well as to those observing the recognition.

Leaders who have the ability to perceive the various parts which make up a whole – for example, noticing individuals (and their contributions) within and outside of one`s immediate circle, department, culture, country, or system – fosters an appreciation of each person, his/her role, and his/her relationship to the group- the team, the community, the family, the organization, the country, the world...

As you may guess, the challenge is that not all leaders are systems thinkers, and not all people (leaders included) see the value in people, never mind see equal value in people. Unless leaders and those they lead are ready to change how they think, no amount of training, or preaching, or strong-arming, or rules can create positive change. When how we value people is grounded in our heritage, our religious beliefs, our personal attitudes and mindsets, and/or when how we think is controlled by someone or something perceived to be more powerful than we are, changing those mindsets and habits can be very nearly impossible. But it is possible.

Golden Rule Civility Statesmen learn to recognize readiness in others. They learn to seek potential and the learn how to support others' use of their gifts. After the gifts are identified, recognizing, and honoring contributions based on the gifts is the next step.

Traditionally, recognition for contributions to a workplace is associated with a monetary reward - a gift certificate, a pay raise, a bonus check, or best of all, a promotion. In communities and not for profit organizations, recognition often takes the form of badges, or ribbons, and some public honoring or award ceremony. While there is nothing wrong with any these rewards, what differentiates great leaders from ordinary leaders, or even good leaders, is a clear understanding that appreciating others is very different from recognizing them. Recognition without true appreciation doesn't always have the impact one might hope.

When you have Recognition + Appreciation/value you get Honor. Honor is a critical aspect of building trust and civility.

To clarify this point, consider Merriam-Webster online dictionary definitions: Recognize: to acknowledge formally Appreciate: to value or admire highly.

But, according to vocabulary.com, "If you APPRECIATE something, you RECOGNIZE its value." So, to recognize is to acknowledge existence. To appreciate is to attach value to the existence.

Research shows that when we observe reverence, appreciation and honor bestowed on others, it impacts us at an emotional and sometimes chemical level. Research also shows that our personal emotional and physical strength is impacted by perceptions of incivility/poor people treatment,[21] e.g. Think about how well you function, and how well you are able to concentrate or focus on a task, after you have experienced a rude comment, or someone has cut you off when driving, or said something unkind. Moreover, when you feel upset, do you want to reach out and help others? Impact includes lack of trust, withdrawal, increased disengagement, difficulty maintaining relationships, less involvement in social, civic and community events… And more incivility, in a cycle.

Have you ever been recognized for something, but the recognition felt hollow because you didn't feel appreciated? If so, when? And, what could those rewarding you have done or said to make you feel honored?

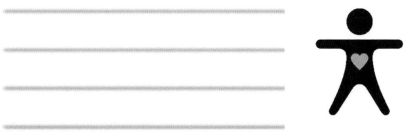

---

[21] From National Civility Center Online Civility Ambassador Course. LB. Adapted from Pearson and Porath

There have been countless recognition mechanisms set in motion around the world related to awarding athletes, politicians, celebrities, authors, creatives, etc., however, when these awards are presented without considering the overall impact and influence that an individual has, and without considering whether the award recipients are good examples of positive people treatment, we send the wrong messages to our children and to each other. Recognizing leaders in any field, sector, talent or skill area without considering how that treatment reflects on ourselves and others is irresponsible.

Consideration of 'Treat others the way you want to be treated,' is the true change agent. Without this element, of Golden Rule Universal People Treatment, individuals will continue to focus on inequalities and our societies will continue to hate and degrade each other. We often fail to recognize that there are ramifications to not applying Golden Rule People Treatment. And when we do this, history tells us the story... history shows us how has people mistreatment affected the ending of so many lives. Those that suffer from the hand of incivility as well as those who continue to behave uncivilly.

For a partial listing (entries are added ongoing) of individuals and organizations striving to exhibit positive people treatment, visit www.goldenrulecivility.com and click on the Directory. There are literally 100s of individuals and organizations engaging in activities and initiatives that are in some way related to The Golden Rule or Civility.

According to Dr. Clyde Rivers, *"We've learned that it is a part of our very human nature to desire for appreciation, one of our most basic needs. When we consider the principles of civility, that we must be constantly aware of and acknowledge our impact on others. The connection between the human desire to be appreciated and civility becomes very clear. When we acknowledge and appreciated the actions and deeds of others we are applying civility principals. We are acting civilly when we show our application to a co-worker, family member, or stranger for helping us out".*

Ambassador Fidelia Graand-Galon – Republic of Suriname South America. This lady has poured out her life to the people of the Caribbean, especially her country Suriname. She is an advocate for women and the Maroon people. She is a Golden Rule Intl. World Peace Ambassador.

Just What Is Honoring Someone?

To honor someone is a form of kindness- specifically, it is an aspect of Human-kindness. When Dr. Lew Bayer, Co-founder of the Golden Rule Civility Global Initiative states (as has been her personal mantra for almost 20 years) that "Civility is its own reward", she is highlighting this attitude of generosity that underpins true civility. To recognize someone, and then to honor them as a way of showing you appreciate them, is a tremendous kindness. In extending this kindness, you are showing people they have value, that their behavior and choices have not gone unnoticed and that they have impacted you in some important way.

Another outcome of honoring someone, is that frequently you can elevate a person's perception of self-worth. In addition, people tend to reciprocate this kind of kindness, often by "paying it forward", either through words or action extended to someone else.

Think about a time when someone has been unexpectedly kind to you and asked for nothing in return. Write some examples here.

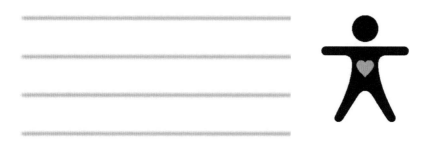

_____

_____

_____

_____

When have you been kind to someone else and expected nothing in return?

_____

_____

_____

_____

iChange Nations™ with its collaborative partners have implemented an International Honorary Award infrastructure to empower and equip our citizens and alumni members with the tools needed to effectively pursue and transform the world. Their Elite Global Network is our greatest asset, consisting of individuals who can implement conflict resolutions and policies to all nations, governments and communities throughout the world.

Some examples of ways you could perform a random act of kindness[22]:

- Let somebody into the better parking space
- Help someone to get something that is out of their reach
- Stop to make sure that everyone is alright at the scene of a break-down or accident
- Hold the door open for someone
- Give up your seat for someone
- Take the time to visit someone who is shut in
- Make eye contact with the homeless person holding the sign -- offer them food
- Volunteer at a soup kitchens
- Leave a *really* good tip
- Smile at someone
- Hold your tongue when you are angry

Write down your own ideas for small kindnesses you can extend to others.

[22] Source: from Module 3 "Articles" in Civility Ambassador ppt project - 7 Habits of Considerate People By Alena Hall (Sept 3, 2014). Healthy Living: Huffington Post

Sydney Allicock – Vice President of Indigenous People Affairs – Guyana, South America. He is working with the indigenous people of Guyana in skills training to produce jobs. His goal is to eradicate poverty for indigenous people around the world.

What did you take away from the section about The Golden Rule? Make a note of ideas, and concepts you'd like to remember. Don't forget to write a personal goal statement for something you will do, learn or change.

"Never be happy with an A+ grade in an obsolete system" - Dr. Clyde Rivers

KEY CONCEPT 7: GOLDEN RULE CIVILITY STATESMEN

Golden Rule Civility Statesman™

A Golden Rule Civility Statesman is a change agent. Statesmen are skilled behavior engineers who will establish The Golden Rule Civility Culture where people treatment is the focal point as viewed through the lens of The Golden Rule.

– Golden Rule Civility Global Initiative

iChange Nations™ (ICN) Founder and President as well as the Golden Rule Dialogue Expert, Dr. Clyde Rivers along with Dr. Donella Pitzl and their team have a mandate to bring Golden Rule Honor, train Statesman to help humanity and create avenues for Golden Rule Civility and Dialogue around the world. They continue to bring their message to governments, law enforcement, communities, tribes, and nations. They work tirelessly and selflessly to make others great around them, a Golden Rule example for the whole world. In 2017, ICN partnered with the team at Civility Experts Inc. who have been internationally recognized as leaders in civility training for almost 20 years. The team led by Dr. Lew Bayer, has discovered that there are measurable competencies that underpin an individual's ability to be civil. That civility is recognized as a true skill and not a "soft" skill is incredibly important as it is this concept that has provided the tools and curriculum, that those who endorse the Golden Rule need, in order to put their beliefs about people treatment into action.

The original concept of a "Statesman" has always included key attributes and abilities such as: e.g., honor, respect, restraint, accountability, responsibility, and generosity. However, it is not always easy to measure these qualities or explain to someone who doesn't come by them naturally how to acquire them. As such, the Golden Rule Civility Initiative collaborators, ICN and Civility Experts looked at the research, reviewed what has made the "Statesmen" identified by ICN "honorable", and also looked at what leadership qualities have supported successful workplace civility initiatives. In this process some patterns emerged and twelve core areas of knowledge, skills and abilities that Golden Rule Civility Statesmen need to be successful were identified. These are scaffolding skills, and are indicated on the Golden Rule Civility Competency Pyramid graphic. Each of these skills is essential to a Statesman's ability to teach, build, support, and lead interruptions and create cultures of honor.

THINK ABOUT IT: How do you currently exhibit key attributes and abilities of a Golden Rule Civility Statesman e.g., honor, respect, restraint, accountability, responsibility, generosity.

General Information About the Twelve Golden Rule Civility Competencies

LEVEL 1: General

Change Readiness

- Relates to the capacity to learn and to think differently, and to do so continuously.

Golden Rule Philosophy

-Relates to knowledge and acceptance of the concept of "doing unto others as you would have done unto you," as a personal standard and a way of being in the world.

Social Intelligence

-Relates to the ability to develop and use one's social radar, social style, and social knowledge to interrelate and interact successfully with others.

Collaboration

-Relates to the capacity to work will with others and contribute to a shared purpose, even when the benefits to oneself are unknown or perceived as unequal to the benefits of other collaborators.

Communicating Respect

-Relates to the ability to convey respect and consideration for others through one's verbal, nonverbal and tonal communication.

Speaking Skills

-Relates to the capacity to deliver compelling, persuasive, and inspirational messages, through presentations or through training that compel others to think differently and/or to take action.

Cultural Competence

-Relates to the capacity to accept and build on perceived differences, without necessarily understanding all the nuances of individual cultures.

Systems Thinking

-Relates to knowledge of systems and how the various parts of a system impact, and are impacted, and how to interpret and in some cases devise interruptions to feedback loops.

LEVEL 2- Master

Media- Creating and Managing

-Relates to the need to monitor, manage, and create positive change messaging while working in partnership with media.

Verbal Engineering

-Relates to the capacity to re-frame key messaging into terms and verbiage that is meaningful to specific audiences based on their respective frames of reference.

Customizing Your Script

-Relates to the ability to adapt core messaging to address the needs of various stakeholders.

Designing A Culture of Honor

-Relates to having an understanding of what honor looks like in different contexts and cultures amidst chronic change and diverse expectations of stakeholders.

What Does Golden Rule Civility Statesman Action Look Like?

Nelson Mandela, is a globally recognized activist and advocate for human rights. Mandela lead several peaceful protests and armed resistance in South Africa during the apartheid years. Mandela was imprisoned for over thirty years, became the face of the anti apartheid movement, and in 1994 became the first black president of South Africa. Mandela remained a champion of peace and social justice worldwide for the rest of his life. These are the actions of a Golden Rule Civility Statesmen.

Dr. Donella Pitzl, Executive Director of Global Operations for ICN states, *"According to our experience in building Statesmen, these are quality people, not unlike President Mandela , that are not swayed by popular voice, as a politician is, but rather these individuals have deep-seated beliefs and an understanding of how to help the world. Statesmen are dedicated to their purpose and selflessness in working to bring the world to a better place. We have trained many Statesman who are involved in global initiatives that are reforming how the world looks at honor and people treatment. Statesmen are changing the world around them"*.

Mussie Hailu - Founder of the Golden Rule Initiative and one of the world's top Philanthropists. He is one of the world's top activists for the Golden Rule developing and propagating the message of the Golden Rule around the globe.

What did you take away from the section about The Golden Rule? Make a note of ideas, and concepts you'd like to remember. Don't forget to write a personal goal statement for something you will do, learn or change.

KEY CONCEPT 8: INTERRUPTION STRATEGIES

"It takes a true interruption to change systems, interruptions cause you to stop and pay attention"
– Dr. Donella Pitzl

Interruption Strategies®

Approaches and techniques used to stop ineffective, unproductive or uncivil behavior and thinking patterns.

– Golden Rule Civility Global Initiative

Ultimately, the goal of the training that Golden Rule Civility Statesmen receive is that it will enable them to be change-makers. High capacity leaders, authors and change agents ("influencers") all have the ability to anticipate, and offset or mitigate, problems before they happen, and to predict or expect outcomes of change. When we talk about Golden Rule Civility we reference "interrupters" – Interrupters are influencers/change agents. Interrupting incivility is an important phase in the 5 Step Golden Rule Civility Change Initiative Cycle.

Golden Rule Civility Statesmen are "interrupters" who are able to foresee what's ahead and to predict an outcome if things do NOT change.

Interrupters understand the relationship between cause and effect and know how to leverage their understanding and experience to think things through. They anticipate outcomes based on each situation so that they can respond strategically to get the results they wish to achieve.

The Golden Rule Civility Global Initiative - Opportunities for Effective Interruption

"Interruption Strategies®" are approaches and techniques used to stop ineffective, unproductive or uncivil behavior and thinking patterns. Interruptions could be as simple as simply disallowing an inappropriate conversation to continue or they can be more complex, such as working for years to have a government policy changed.

There are many situations in which you can make a difference. Being an interrupter means being willing to make, and exemplify change, (you do this through your words or actions). As a change-maker, you have the intention to interrupt the "usual" and instead reach for something better. While it may seem simple, e.g., see something bad, decide to change it and take action, the reality is that lasting change is not always easy.

Effective interrupters are deliberate and strategic in how they create change. Yes, sometimes the action is spontaneous and based on intuition or experience, but it is always important to consider the impacts and implications of change and to do so while focusing on others- this versus seeking acknowledgement, or power or notoriety.

How do you know when an interruption is the right course of action?

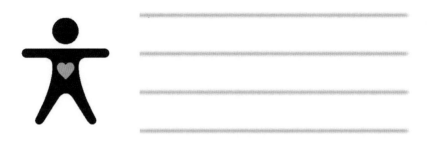

If you consider that incivility and people treatment can be interrupted at all levels of life, e.g., at home, at school, in the community, in workplaces, in the public forum, in sporting events, etc., as well as in larger government and political arenas, can you think of ways you could interrupt?

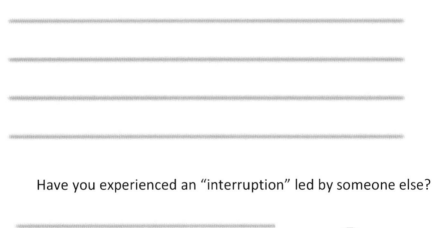

Have you experienced an "interruption" led by someone else?

Steps to Successful Interrupting

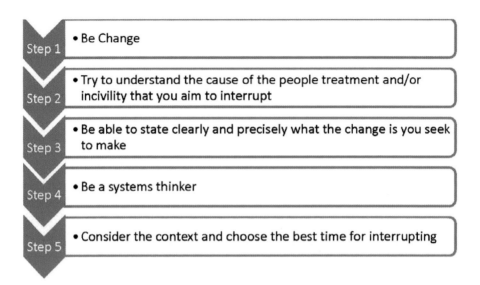

Step 1	• Be Change
Step 2	• Try to understand the cause of the people treatment and/or incivility that you aim to interrupt
Step 3	• Be able to state clearly and precisely what the change is you seek to make
Step 4	• Be a systems thinker
Step 5	• Consider the context and choose the best time for interrupting

Step 1: Be change ready. Seek to learn. Enter into the work of interrupting with an open heart and an open mind. Suspend your perceptions and anticipate that your own beliefs and values may need to shift.

You cannot expect to lead others to change if you are not adaptive and flexible yourself. It is important to consider all the possible factors and situational nuances and influences that could impact an interruption. (e.g., individuals involved in the interruption come and go, political situations, costs/resources, natural disasters, e.g., bad weather the day of a planned march, etc.)

Step 2: Try to understand the cause of the people treatment and/or incivility that you aim to interrupt. Do not make assumptions...ask questions, research, live in the situation, and do everything you can to learn what has enable those exhibiting the people treatment and what the experience is of those on the receiving end of the treatment.

Listen to the history and stories, seek expert advice and opinion.

Step 3: Have a clear end in mind goal, e.g., be able to state clearly and precisely what the change is you seek to make. You can't measure effectiveness without a starting metric, and you won't know if you are successful unless you define success. Ensure that the benefits of the end goal are known and clear to all stakeholders.

Step 4: Be a systems thinker, that is, consider how the interruption might impact or be impacted by people, events, resources, demographics etc. (change doesn't happen in a vacuum).

You must always consider that what seems a useful interruption in one aspect or area or situation, could create a negative and unplanned interruption in another situation, aspect, individual or area.

Step 5: Consider the context and choose the best time for interrupting. All the good intentions in the world, and the best laid plans may be ineffective if those you are interruption are not open to change, if there is low trust, or if there is low engagement – e.g., those you are changing do not understand the benefits of the change.

Once you have properly assessed the situation and you are ready to be a positive influence and interrupt, the next step is identifying the nature of the interruption. There are many approaches and strategies to interrupting. These are taught in the Golden Rule Civility Statesman training.

Think about times in your life when you have "interrupted", that is, when have you stood up and taken action to right a wrong?

Have you ever caused others to stop something they were doing? How did you do it?

_____

_____

_____

_____

What did you take away from the section about The Golden Rule? Make a note of ideas, and concepts you'd like to remember. Don't forget to write a personal goal statement for something you will do, learn or change.

_____

_____

_____

_____

KEY CONCEPT 9: THE GOLDEN RULE QUESTION

"Every life is valuable and created for a contribution to the world" - Dr. Clyde Rivers

The Golden Rule Question®

If you were on the other side of the behavior/treatment, would you want that same treatment?

- Dr. Clyde Rivers

The concept of people treatment has been developed by Dr. Clyde Rivers in his global work building cultures of honor.

Martin Luther King's work during the 1950s and 1960s and through non-violent protests based on the ideals of Ghandi helped the United States' black population gain equal rights. King is largely credited with being one, if not the biggest force, behind the passing of the Civil Rights Act of 1964 and Voting Rights Act (1965) which provided the black American population with increased rights and opportunities.

When we build cultures of honor, one of the key outcomes is positive people treatment. There are many benefits and outcomes of positive people treatment, for example:

- Kindness
- Fairness
- Quality of life
- Peace
- Personal health and safety
- Increased education
- Liberty
- Individual confidence
- Growth opportunities
- Collaboration
- Creativity e.g., individuals can use their gifts
- Happiness

When was the last time you sent someone flowers anonymously, and for no reason except to let that person know that he or she was appreciated?

_____

_____

_____

_____

Can you recall a time recently when you chose to give someone who had wronged you the benefit of the doubt, and offered him or her kindness instead of issuing a barbed comment or demanding an apology?

How often do you take time to do the little extras: set a pretty table, hand- write a thank you card, reach out to a new neighbor, offer a heartfelt compliment, or extend some other seemingly small gesture to make life a little easier for someone else—even when it costs you your own time, money or energy to do so?

What does the voice in your head say to you when you encounter someone who is different than you?

Or, when someone does or says something you don't agree with, do you immediately focus on the person or the action? Do you make assumptions about "why" the person is behaving a certain way? Do you pause to think about the situation, the background, the conditions?

Or, do you quickly pass judgment?

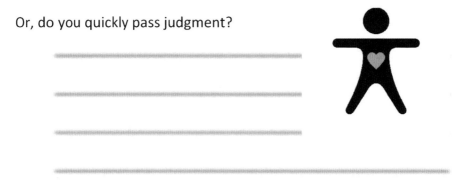

When we encounter situations where there is disagreement, and when diverse perspectives result in conflict, the Golden Rule Philosophy would always encourage us to consider approaching the situation by engaging in civil dialogue. Learning to listen, with the intention of understanding, is not easy. Many leaders, negotiators, peace-makers and others who strive to resolve conflict spend a great deal of time and energy learning how to engage in civil dialogue.

KEY CONCEPT 10: GOLDEN RULE DIALOGUE

Golden Rule Dialogue is communication where the intention is to learn from the diverse perspectives of others, to listen for change, and to gain knowledge for building better systems.

– Golden Rule Civility Global Initiative

Golden Rule Dialogue enables participants to make more efficient and effective decisions that will benefit organizations, individuals, teams, communities, and even countries. Successful Golden Rule Dialogue requires that those participating value honor, civility, peace, and each other. – Dr.Clyde Rivers

iChange Nations Inc. seeks to build cultures of honor, train statesman and create chambers for Golden Rule Dialogue. iChange Nations Inc. is the largest building cultures of honor network around the globe, we are training ICN Statesman to work in their initiatives to help the world and Dr. Rivers is the Golden

Rule Dialogue Expert addressing issues globally and creating dialogue forums.

Managing Uncivil Discourse

Others may be rude, and may make choices you do not approve of. Your job is to carefully choose your thoughts, actions and words – no matter what others do. To do this, it`s important to align closely with your personal values, what you stand for, in deciding moment by moment how you will engage with the world, and with others.

So how do you handle uncivil discourse?

- Always elevate the conversation, and thus lead by example. When someone is negative, find and express the positive, without criticizing the negativity.
- Look for the best everywhere you go, and others will give that to you. If someone is unkind, address it: for example, if someone says something rude about another person, say "I see it differently. She is a fine person." Or "Everyone is doing the best they can – encouragement helps people more than criticism." If someone is rude directly to you, you can: ignore it, smile and keep walking, or, depending on the circumstances, say "That`s not kind. I`m doing the best I can, and that`s good enough for me."

Respect for Policy, the Law, and Government

A key part of civility is knowing and following the social rules in any context. Rules are in place to help everyone get along better, and co-exist within shared places and spaces. It`s helpful for our mutual co-existence, for example, to have and obey traffic laws wherever we are.

If we all follow the rules, we are all collectively safer, and thus we all benefit. Plus, it makes life easier when you have a knowledge of that is appropriate in a specific situation or at a specific time. When we behave appropriately in any given context, according to the rules that are understood by everyone, it makes relationships with others easier because we are all more at ease and comfortable with each other.

Taking time and care to learn the rules in any given context (your workplace, the laws that apply where you are) and then honoring them, is respect – we are showing our respect for the rules themselves (the order they provide) and others (that we care about their well-being and safety) and society (recognizing the importance of order and agreement when we co-exist with many others)

In the Public Forum

Set a good example by honoring the spirit of the laws where you live, and the rules in your workplace. Everyone is more comfortable when they know what to expect from everyone else.

Support your government: And even when you can't wholly support, take time to learn. Ask questions, seek to understand current issues, and different perspectives. Exercise your rights to free speech, the right to vote, and other rights as they may be provided to you. And pay attention to when these rights are not offered equally to everyone- and question that too.

Use civil discourse whenever you are in disagreement. This means practicing restraint and controlling your emotions. This means being accountable to others and being responsible to yourself. Try to see the best in people. Assume good intentions, and try not to judge others.

Remember, respect is something each of us is deserving of

Civility requires accepting that others are different from me, different ideas, experiences, habits, values, cultures and so on. Civility requires that we accept even when we don't understand. And the Golden Rule Philosophy includes an understanding that even when there are differences, there is value- value in the individual, the differences, the ideas, the habits, the experiences and so on.

Consider hosting small meetings or social events where you can invite friends and newcomers, neighbors and acquaintances with differing ideologies and experiences. Get involved in your community. Walk in your neighborhood, get to know people. Re-engage and show interest. Participate in conversations and create dialogue opportunities.

Kenneth Kaunda - Former President of Zambia and a living champion of peace for his country. He was responsible for helping Nelson Mandala in his fight for freedom in South Africa. He successfully united the over 70 tribes in Zambia that are still united to this day. His mantra, "One Zambia, One Nation" He is the 1st recipient of the World Civility Award.

Dialogues are commonly used in public-policy conflicts, international conflicts, and ethnic conflicts to <u>build up mutual understanding and trust</u> between members of opposing groups. They do a great deal to enhance public conversation and transform the way parties interact.

Through dialogue, public discourse can become more complex, inviting, and informative. Those who engage in dialogue may bring their new ways of thinking and relating back to their organizations, friends, families, or citizen groups. They may question derogatory attributions made about their opponent and may work to combat stereotypes in their larger society. They may also be less likely to accept extremist leaders.

When participants are activists, they can influence the organizations at which they work or can affect key decision makers. When parties themselves are leaders, the impact on public discourse may be even more direct and immediate. Although dialogues do not lead directly to resolution, and this is not their immediate goal, they can help parties to develop new understanding that leads to formal negotiations. This paves the way for effective problem solving and increases the possibility of eventual resolution. Constructive public conversations about divisive controversy decreases the costs and dangers typically associated with deep- rooted conflict.

Dialogue also has various transformative effects on relationships. Like transformative mediation, it puts the relational development of disputants ahead of settlement. When people are stuck in protracted conflict, they often view each other as inferior beings with inadequate moral or cognitive capacities. Through dialogue, disputants learn to articulate their own voices clearly and to recognize each other's viewpoints as valid. Disputants honestly express uncertainties about their own position and explore the complexities of the issues being discussed, which can help them to let go of stereotypes, distrust, and reverse patterns of polarization. Thoughts and feelings that are often kept hidden are thus revealed.

Disputants can begin to incorporate their different subjective viewpoints into a shared definition of their different needs, motives, and values. As they become aware of the fears, hopes, and deeply held values of the other participants, parties may begin to trust each other more and feel closer to each other. People begin to realize that they have important things in common, which allows for collective learning, creativity, and an increased sense of fellowship. <u>This can help to create a community-based culture of cooperation, collaboration, partnership, and inclusion.</u>

But in addition to the transformation that takes place at a relational level, dialogue can also transform parties at an individual level. Because participants do not know beforehand what they will say, they must listen not only to one another, but also to themselves. Parties must inquire into what conflict means to them and how their own processes and behavior have negatively shaped the course of conflict. As they begin to express themselves in new ways, they come to better understand their own motives and needs. This sort of interaction makes growth and real learning possible, and allows parties to more fully realize the potential that lies within them. In one sense, the self comes into existence through dialogue[23].

An Example of a Golden Rule Dialogue Initiative - ICN Women of Golden Rule Dialogue™

VISION/MISSION: iChange Nations Inc. believes women of the world have brilliant minds created to bring solutions to the issues around them and the world. It is our intention to create global platforms for women to address global issues and bring

---

[23] Source: Dialogue: beyond Intractability – by Michelle Maise 2003

Golden Rule Solutions, "Treat others the way you want to be treated" in their solutions.

HONOR SYSTEM: iChange Nations™ has an honor system whereby women with outstanding initiatives and philosophies will be acknowledged and awarded the ICN Women of Global Solutions Award. This will allow the world to know of their brilliant ideas and have access to their problem solving Golden Rule solutions.

PLATFORM: Establish Acti-Vention Forums, in collaboration with women from around the globe, bringing their initiatives, addressing issues and finding solutions to global issues.

SOCIAL MEDIA AND MEDIA: iChange Nations™ will use social media and other media outlets to document and publicize these forums to allow the world to tap into the creative, Golden Rule problem solving discussions and have access to engage the ICN Women of Golden Rule Dialogue™ in global discussions.

ABOUT iCHANGE NATIONS™: Dr. Clyde Rivers, Founder and President of iChange Nations™ is a strong advocate for the voice of women around the world. He believes every woman has a gift and contrition that will help make the world a better and more peaceful place for mankind. He believes women carry many of the solutions to help the world and he intends to allow their voices to have a global audience to speak into the issues that need answers and solutions. In addition to this, iChange Nations™ seeks to build cultures of honor, train statesman and create chambers for Golden Rule Dialogue. iChange Nations™ is the largest building cultures of honor network around the globe, we are training ICN Statesman to working in their initiatives to help the world and Dr. Rivers is the Golden Rule Dialogue Expert addressing issues globally and creating dialogue forums.

Community Civility Counts, a partnership between the Gary Chamber of Commerce and The Times Media Co., launched on April 22, 2015, at a news conference in Gary, Indiana.

Chuck Hughes, executive director of the Gary Chamber of Commerce, credits Gordon E. Bradshaw, the chamber's public policy chairman, for bringing the idea forward at a March 2015 committee meeting and for designing a poster.

That poster caught the attention of Ambassador to the United Nations for Interfaith Peace-Building Initiative, Dr. Clyde Rivers of the Golden Rule International and President and Founder of iChange Nations Inc. The Times Media Co. provides a platform for the movement through Facebook, Twitter, Instagram and the hashtag #civilitycount

What did you take away from the section about The Golden Rule? Make a note of ideas, and concepts you'd like to remember. Don't forget to write a personal goal statement for something you will do, learn or change

Golden Rule Civility
Personal Action Plan

Action I Will Take	Date I Will Take Action	Supports I Need to Complete the Action	Benefits to Me, Others, and The World

The TEN KEYS to GOLDEN RULE CIVILITY

Treat others how you would like to be treated

Let civility be its own reward

Acknowledge each other's gifts and equal value

Commit to positive people treatment

Work together consciously and strategically

Recognize that shifting culture is a long-term change initiative

Honor each other

Build Golden Rule Civility competency continuously

Find the courage to interrupt incivility

Engage in civil dialogue

Test Yourself

1. According to ICN, Statesmen can be described as people who:
   a) are not swayed by popular voice
   b) have a deep-seated belief and understanding on how to help the world
   c) are dedicated to their purpose
   d) display selflessness in working to bring the world to a better place
   e) all of the above.

2. What are some of the results of people mistreatment?
   a) it eventually affects those who are mistreating others
   b) decreased productivity
   c) lowered self esteem
   d) better profitability
   e) a, b, and c

3. To manage uncivil discourse, you need to:
   a) know your values and align with them
   b) choose well, no matter what others do
   c) try to be right as often as possible
   d) a and b

4. What would be a symptom of incivility?
   a) interrupting
   b) swearing
   c) racism
   d) all of the above

5. Etiquette and civility:
   a) are the same
   b) are different-etiquette depends on your personal

values and civility does not

- c) are different – civility is based on your personal values and etiquette is not
- d) none of these

6. What is not true of the Golden Rule?
   - a) it first originated with the Christian Bible
   - b) it is a universal moral principle that has many variations around the world
   - c) it means trying to empathize with other people, including those who may be very different from us
   - d) it means people should try to treat each other as they would like to be treated themselves – with tolerance, consideration, and compassion

7. What is not true about values?
   - a) in becoming aware of our own values, we can more easily see and understand the values that may be guiding others' behavior
   - b) values do not influence people`s behaviors
   - c) values are principles or standards of behavior - one's judgment of what is important in life:
   - d) often values are contained within the meanings of famous sayings and proverbs.
   - e) a and b

8. Thinking about another`s perspective is called:
   - a) kindness
   - b) empathy
   - c) intelligent
   - d) none of these

9. When others are rude at work, civility asks us to:
   - a) be rude back, but only if they really deserve it
   - b) take responsibility for getting back at them

c) take responsibility for our own thoughts and actions
d) hold the employer fully responsible for handling the problem.

10. Respect:
   a) means acknowledging another person`s humanity
   b) means acknowledging people are worthy of being treated with dignity
   c) requires accountability
   d) involves being non-judgmental
   e) all of the above

"The next great idea leads the way" - *Dr. Clyde Rivers*

GOLDEN RULE CIVILITY SOURCES AND RESOURCES

Recommend Reading

- *Respecting our Differences* by Lynn Duvall
- *Honest Direct Respectful – Three Simple Words That Will Change Your Life* by Dennis Adams
- *Mastering Respectful Confrontation* by Joe Weston
- *Respectful Parents Respectful Kids* by Sura Hart Victoria Kindle Hodson
- *The Respect Virus: How to Create a Contagious Culture of Respect* by Diane Windingland
- *The Power of Civility*, collected authors, available at www.powerofcivility.com
- *The Civility Solution* by Dr. P. Forni
- *The Thinking Life* by Dr. P. Forni
- *Power from Within* by Dr. Danita Johnson Hughes
- *Road to Respect: Path to Profit* by Erica Pinsky
- *Social Intelligence: The New Science of Human Relationships* by Daniel Goleman
- *Just Listen* by Mark Goulston M.D.
- *The Lost Art of Listening, Second Edition: How Learning to Listen Can Improve Relationships* by Michael P. Nichols, Ph.D.
- *The Power of Now* by Eckhart Tolle
- *The Speed of Trust* by Stephan Covey
- *The Thin Book of Trust an Essential Primer for Building Trust at Work* by Charles Feltman
- *Virtue as Social Intelligence* by Nancy Snow
- *Crucial Conversations* by Patterson and Grenny
- *51 Activities for Collaborative Management* by Peter Garber
- *First Impressions: What You Don't Know About How Others See You* - by Ann Demarais, Ph.D. and Valerie White, PhD.
- *The Fifth Discipline: The Art and Practice of the Learning*

Organization by Peter Senge
- *John Sterman's Business Dynamics: Systems Thinking and Modeling for a Complex World*
- *The Complete Problem Solver* by John D. Arnold, John D
- *Systems Thinking for Social Change -A Practical Guide to Solving Complex Problems, Avoiding Unintended Consequences, and Achieving Lasting Results* by David Peter Stroh
- *A Leadership Paradox: Influencing Others by Defining Yourself* by Greg Robinson

Recommended Websites, News Articles, Videos
- http://www.values.com/respect - RESPECT
- http://www.ehow.com/info_12120048_10-ways-show-respect-adults.html 10 WAYS TO TEACH RESPECT TO ADULTS
- http://www.teach-nology.com/tutorials/teaching/respect/ HOW TO TEACH AND SHOW RESPECT
- http://wiki.answers.com/Q/What_is_the_importance_of_having_respect_for_others IMPORTANCE OF RESPECTING OTHERS
- http://www.wikihow.com/Respect-Yourself
- http://www.littlethingsmatter.com/blog/2010/10/07/personal-accountability%E2%80%94a- requirement-for-life-advancement/
- http://www.mindtools.com/pages/article/taking-responsibility.htm
- http://www.mindtools.com/pages/article/taking-responsibility.htm
- Rude Behavior at Work is Increasing and Affects the Bottom Line by Thunderbird School of Management 2013
- https://www.sciencedaily.com/releases/2013/01/130130184048.htm

- Civility by Amanda Horne 2013
- http://positivepsychologynews.com/news/amanda-horne/2013041025769
- The Ethics of the Future by Jostein Gaarder in Huffington Post http://www.huffingtonpost.com/jostein-gaarder/ethics-future_b_8576266.html
- Ten Tips for Creating Respect and Civility in Your Workplace by Barbara Richman 2014 http://www.lorman.com/resources/ten-tips-for-creating-respect-and-civility-in-your- workplace-15463
- Why the Golden Rule Must be Practiced in Business by Brenton Hayden https://www.entrepreneur.com/topic/golden-rule

Courses
- http://www.lessonplanet.com/search?keywords=Activities+that+Teach+Respect&type_ids%5B
- %5D=357918&type_ids%5B%5D=357922&gclid=CLjT6pSk_70CFecWMgodp0QAHw
- http://www.micheleborba.com/Pages/BMI05.htm activities x35+
- http://therespectdare.com/e-course e-course
- http://www.osca.com/courses/human-resources/preventing-workplace-harassment-respect-in-the-workplace-(employees).aspx
- http://www.diversityresources.com/hr-training.htm
- http://www.lessonplanet.com/search?keywords=Activities+that+Teach+Respect&type_ids%5B
- %5D=357918&type_ids%5B%5D=357922&gclid=CLjT6pSk_70CFecWMgodp0QAHw
- http://www.micheleborba.com/Pages/BMI05.htm activities x35+
- http://therespectdare.com/e-course e-course
- http://www.osca.com/courses/human-

resources/preventing-workplace-harassment-respect-in-
the-workplace-(employees).aspx
- http://www.diversityresources.com/hr-training.htm

Videos

- A Call for Civility
https://www.youtube.com/watch?v=bXOObdcUmNU
- What is Civility?
https://www.youtube.com/watch?v=dLNd1AuCpBg
- The Golden Rule
https://www.youtube.com/watch?v=2Ci613QcC5E
- The Golden Rule (Children)
https://www.youtube.com/watch?v=d56rsXJ86Yw
- 5 Steps for being Present by Michael Formica (2011)
https://www.psychologytoday.com/blog/enlightened-
living/201106/5-steps-being-present
- Eckhart Tolle: Being in the Present Moment
https://www.youtube.com/watch?v=xvkuP3e_Uvk
- Deepak Chopra: Being Present
https://www.youtube.com/watch?v=84yK5sj8X50
- Do Good Deeds with Kindness, Compassion and Love
https://www.youtube.com/watch?v=- QZhoREVxfw
- One person makes the Difference. The power of One
https://www.youtube.com/watch?v=RjZwmsCLwMc
- 7 Habits of Considerate People
http://www.huffingtonpost.com/2014/08/27/habits-of-
considerate-people_n_5710033.html
- Active Listening: Hear What People are Really Trying to say
- https://www.mindtools.com/CommSkll/ActiveListening.htm
- Three Tips to Help You Disagree Politely (Meghan Overdeep)
http://www.southernliving.com/culture/disagreements-
arguments-tips-tricks
- Many people are Reaching Out Across the Partisan Divide
After Trump's Election

http://www.civilpolitics.org/content/many-people-are-reaching-out-across-the-partisan-divide- after-trumps-election/
- YouTube: https://www.ted.com/talks/howard_rheingold_on_collaboration
- https://www.danielbranch.com/respect-yourself-and-others/
- https://hbr.org/2013/01/the-price-of-incivility
- http://www.huffingtonpost.com/anne-loehr/how-to-live-with-purpose-_b_5187572.html
- http://www.independent.co.uk/news/science/how-to-convince-some-to-change-their-mind- according-to-science-a6867291.html
- 25 Speeches Discussing Current Global Issues - https://www.trendhunter.com/course/global- issues-speech

Other Resources

- Recommended – online quiz at: www.clearthinking.org http://www.clearerthinking.org/the-political-bias-test
- Civilpolitics.org:
- Educating the Public on Evidence-based methods for improving inter-group civility
- http://www.civilpolitics.org/
- Resource: Living Room Conversations
- http://www.livingroomconversations.org/
- Philosophy: In today's world, we often find ourselves unable to connect with people of
- differing perspectives. Not understanding each other has led to dehumanizing others in a way that is detrimental to our society as a whole. This has led to our increased polarization and political gridlock.
- Living Room Conversations are a simple way that anyone with an open mind can engage with their friends in a friendly yet meaningful conversation about topics we care

about. These conversations increase understanding, reveal common ground and allow us to discuss possible solutions. No fancy event or skilled facilitator is needed.

- When people of all walks of life begin to care about one another, they can begin working together to solve the wicked problems of our time.
- Living Room Conversations is an open source project. Please use, share and modify with attribution to www.LivingRoomConversations.org
- Civility Matters! An Evidence-based Review on How to Cultivate a Respectful Federal Public Service
- http://www.apex.gc.ca/uploads/key%20priorities/health/civility%20report%20%20 eng.pdf

Quiz Answers: (page 129)

1. E
2. E
3. D
4. D
5. C
6. A
7. B
8. B
9. C
10. E